ST. AUGUSTINE
by Rebecca West

A Thomas More Book to Live
THE THOMAS MORE PRESS
Chicago, Illinois

This **Thomas More Press Book to Live** edition published in 1982 by the **Thomas More Press,** 225 West Huron Street, Chicago, Illinois 60610, U.S.A., is reprinted by arrangement with Literistic Ltd.

PREFACE

NOBODY could be more conscious than myself of the omissions in this volume. I am especially conscious that I have said very little of Augustine's philosophy, of the implications and influence of *The City of God,* and of his doctrine of the Church as a rule of faith. But a full discussion of these matters would make a very large instead of a very small book; and they have been discussed elsewhere, often with talent and sometimes with genius, while there is still room for a simple account of Augustine's personal life and background.

R. W.

I

Seventeen hundred years ago Cyprian, Bishop of Carthage, took up his pen to explain to the Pro-Consul of Africa why he was wrong in supposing that the Christians' refusal to worship the gods was the reason for the wars and famines and pestilences then vexing the world. First he chastised his correspondent as the Fathers of the Church were wont to chastise the pagan. 'I have often, Demetrianus,' he wrote, 'treated with contempt your railing and noisy clamour with sacrilegious mouth and impious words against the one and true God, thinking it more modest and better silently to scorn the ignorance of a mistaken man than by speaking to provoke the fury of a senseless man. We are, moreover, bidden to keep what is holy within our own knowledge and not expose it to be trodden down by swine and dogs.' After much hearty thwacking of this sort he went on to propound a theory very strange to find in a man of naturally cheerful temperament and not ungratified ambitions.

'You have said,' he wrote, 'that to us should

be attributed the calamities by which the world is now shaken and distressed, because your gods are not now worshipped by us. Now, since you are ignorant of divine knowledge and a stranger to truth, you must in the first place realise this, that the world has now grown old, and does not abide in that strength in which it formerly stood. This we would know, even if the sacred Scriptures had not told us of it, because the world itself announces its approaching end by its failing powers. In the winter there is not so much rain for nourishing the seeds, and in the summer the sun gives not so much heat for ripening the harvest. In springtime the young corn is not so joyful, and the autumn fruit is sparser. Less and less marble is quarried out of the mountains, which are exhausted by their disembowelments, and the veins of gold and silver are dwindling day by day. The husbandman is failing in the fields, the sailor at sea, the soldier in the camp. Honesty is no longer to be found in the market-place, nor justice in the law-courts, nor good craftsmanship in art, nor discipline in morals. Think you that anything which is old can preserve the same powers that it possessed in the prime vigour of its youth? Whatever is tending towards its decay and going to meet its end must needs weaken.

Hence the setting sun sends out rays that hardly warm or cheer, the waning moon is a pale crescent, the old tree that once was green and hung with fruit grows gnarled and barren, and every spring in time runs dry. This is the sentence that has been passed on the earth, this is God's decree: that everything which has had a beginning shall have an end, that everything which has flourished shall fall, that strong things shall become weak, and great things shall become small, and that when they have weakened and dwindled they shall be no more. So no one should wonder nowadays that everything begins to fail, since the whole world is failing, and is about to die.'

So it seemed, seventeen hundred years ago, to many citizens of the Roman Empire. The individual might be full of life—it must indeed have taken a considerable degree of vitality for Cyprian to address in such terms an important representative of the government which not only possessed the power to put him to death but was ready to exercise it, as it actually did some years later—but he felt as if he were suspended in a medium of death. All was going very ill in the Empire. Rome, whose greatness had developed out of a peasant state, had passed on to feudal capitalism, until the domination of

the landowners and business men was smashed
by the joint revolt of the bourgeoisie and the
proletariat. In the new state that followed, the
bourgeoisie waxed fat and fell into the sin of
pride, and ground the faces of the poor; so presently the Empire consisted of rich townsmen
and their dependants on one hand, and hungry
peasants on the other. But even hungry peasants make better soldiers than townsmen, and
the Emperors took them into their armies. At
length there came to be an army which knew
itself solidly peasant, and more peasant than
army. So in the third century there was civil
war between army and bourgeoisie; and since
the proletariat had had no chance of assimilat-
ing the culture of the upper classes, they were
unable to frame a policy of deliverance, and
anarchy was the result.

Order was restored; but it was, rather, a
stabilised disorder. During the century after
Cyprian's death there accumulated more and
more of what he would have taken as evidence
of the world's impending doom. Civilisation
slowed down, it seemed about to stop. There
was still the material substance of the Empire,
the ground to tread, the seas to sail, the fields
where corn and olives could be grown, the
hills where ores could be quarried. But the

roads were falling into ruin, and the seas were vexed by pirates. Agriculture, through heavy taxation both in money and kind and forced labour, was falling into a rapid decay, for which later puzzled historians tried to account by a mythical exhaustion of the soil. Raw materials went unused because the purchasing power of the community was shrinking. Prices soared, and at the same time currency fell; and a mob of tax-collectors who were licensed brigands skinned the remnants of the moneyed classes. There could be no social unity. This disorder gave every class reason to hate all other classes as if they were enemies from another land. Now the army had lost its identity with the peasants, and it hated and was hated by all.

But the age held worse than this. Poverty is a condition which nations can endure; and the Roman Empire was merely returning to the simple agricultural economy from which it had risen. Moreover, it is probably true that innumerable Roman citizens knew little of what was happening to them, for it was still the policy of the Emperors to bribe the urban populations by beautifying the cities, organising public amusement, and distributing doles of corn and oil and wine and bacon. It is hardly credible to us that the vast Baths of Diocletian, a minor chamber of which now makes the Carthusians a spacious church, could have been built when the social and economic structure of the Empire had already collapsed; and it must have been much less credible to those who enjoyed its unruined splendours and had every reason for persuading themselves that such good glutting prosperity must inevitably be permanent. But however much the material disasters of the situation might be concealed from the common man, he had suffered a spiritual mischance which, even if he could not recognise it for what it was, must needs have caused him pain and despair. He had been castrated of his will.

In the old days the Roman Empire had given its children considerable freedom in exchange for their submission to the essential discipline necessary for the maintenance of the State. A peasant of sufficient intelligence and enterprise could become a landowner and rise right through the ranks of society to the senatorial aristocracy; and any meritorious family would have no difficulty in achieving the same feat in a few generations. Even common soldiers had considerable opportunities for advancement, and if a slave could win his freedom—and this was often achieved—there was nothing to prevent him or his children from entering the municipal aristocracy. But, paradoxically enough, the civil wars provoked by the clash between the city bourgeoisie and the peasant army put an end to this social elasticity. The reforms of Diocletian and Constantine were the legislative experiments of men who had been imperfectly educated in the bases of the old Roman civilisation and whose personal experiences had been too constantly preoccupied with violence and compulsion. Hence they treated the organic as if it were the inorganic, and made every man a peg stuck in a hole. Whether he was born in town or country, he found himself committed to an occupation and a domicile which he could not change. It might be that he was lucky enough to be born into the caste, now in practice hereditary, of public officials; but his luck consisted chiefly of the power to grow rich by corruption and extortion. Numerically it was more probable that he would be born into the ranks of the despoiled, where he would not dare show unusual capacity lest he should be compulsorily raised to the *curia,* a dreadful honour, since the *curiales* were corporately responsible with their goods and persons for the taxes of a whole area. It was true that the proletariat in the streets had their bread

and their circuses, but they had no political
rights and they had less and less work and
money. They had the strictly limited and not
satisfying freedom of stray cats to ravage dust-
bins and fight in alleys. Nowhere was there any
release for creative energy. Man could not use
time in the only way it can serve him; he had
no chance to devise a drama in which he could
play his part and reveal the character of his self.
Since he needed that revelation for his own en-
lightenment, since without it he goes out of the
world knowing no more than the beasts of the
field of anything beyond his sensations, it was
as if his life had been cancelled, as if he had
been unfairly given over to death while his flesh
still promised him preservation from it. So the
children of that age sat in an anguished lethargy.

There was but one force which could help
them, and that was Christianity. Before the
civil wars this faith had gathered many adherents from the oppressed proletariat, who were
happy to think that though they were despised
by the possessor classes they were the close and
kindly treated friends of the Son of God; from
the people whose ethical fastidiousness led them
to desire some of that peculiar and delicate wisdom which is only learned in defeat, and which
was too largely lacking in the counsels of Rome;

and from the people who, being of that temperament which finds pleasure in joining movements, were swept into the Church by the pros-
elytising force of St. Paul and his successors.
But as conditions grew worse, Christianity exer-
cised a far wider appeal. At its altar the common man found what was wholly wanting in
the secular world: a sense of the uniqueness and
preciousness of his individuality. Out of his
relationship with his God and his Church he
could devise the needed drama in which he
could play his part and reveal the character of
his self. He was given back the will which
society had cut from him, he was alive after all.
Like an ill dream at the moment of waking, his
anguished lethargy fell from him, and he leaped
up into the day.

This service done by Christianity to the age
produced two conspicuous results. One was the
abandonment of the masses to the pleasures of
religious controversy to an unprecedented degree. It is possible that this degree has been
exaggerated in our minds because we derive our
knowledge of it from the reports of those who
were themselves fanatically interested in such
controversy, and it is the habit of fanatics to
believe that the whole world shares their ob-
sessions. But the disorders that occurred at

certain crises of doctrinal dispute show that, without doubt, enough of the population could become sufficiently excited about such subtle questions as whether the Father and the Son were of the same or like but distinct substance, for the peace of great cities to be endangered. It seems certain that a large section of the community were as familiar with theological matters as, say, English public school boys are today with the main facts relating to automobiles. This led inevitably to comic fatuities of the sort that Gibbon loved to mock, and to the depreciation of thought by the hasty and facile processes inevitable in group-thinking. But since Christian theology had grown out of Greek philosophy and Hebrew ethics and poetry, and since it dealt with the most important movements of the mind, this preoccupation of the community gave every individual a stimulating education and first-rate material on which to use his wits.

The other important result of Christianity's hold over the age was due to the tendency of men to call on the Church to free them from their material pains as it had freed them from their spiritual impotence. This naturally became more marked after Constantine had made it the official religion of the Roman Empire; he

was possibly inspired in his action by the hope
that the Christians' unique power of organisation would enable them to do this very thing.
Hence the thinkers of that age found themselves
forced into a position unlike that occupied by
the thinkers of any other age. They were inevitably attracted by the Church. There was
hardly scope for an original mind outside the
Church; that is proven in the pages of history
by the transference, so swift and complete as
to be dramatic, of all the enduring names from
the pagan records to the tables of the Fathers
of the Church. But once they were inside the
Church, and busy formulating their conceptions
of the universe, they were thrust into the thick
of practical affairs. The bishop who was inves-
tigating the mystery of the Trinity was forced
to assume most of the functions of a Roman
magistrate, and stand between the masses and
the bureaucracy in the position of a popular
tribune. But he was not able to abandon his
speculative thought. He was obliged to go on
formulating his conceptions, because he believed that his ultimate salvation, the inspiration for his practical performances, and his prestige among men were all derived from that
source. The pursuit of the fixed truth remained
his first duty, yet he had continually to prac-

tise the most agile opportunism. This division
and conflict of function must occur whenever a
Church exercises temporal power, or even whenever it attains great importance as a spiritual
institution. But it is doubtful whether it has
ever occurred more picturesquely than it did in
the third and fourth centuries, or raised more
tremendous issues in the lives of single individuals.

Into this world, on Sunday the thirteenth of
November, in the year 354 A.D., at a town named
Thagaste in the Roman province of Numidia,
which is now Souk Ahras in Algeria, there was
born the great genius Augustine. To meet the
unequalled strains and excitements of the age
he brought an unequalled power. That power
he derived from Africa, that stony yet not in-
fertile land, which engendered tremendous
crops, tremendous men, violent events. Though
it was but two days' sail from Tiber mouth, the
Romans looked on it as a land of mystery. Even
after they had foully murdered their Punic enemies there, it seemed as if an enemy remained.
Even when they covered the countryside with
camps and factories, cornfields and olive groves,
they felt an undispelled wonder in the place,
which they conveyed by telling travellers' tales
and peopling it with lions that understood lan-

guage and snakes that banded together to turn back the legions. Perhaps this was because North Africa was edged by the blackness of the unexplored. But perhaps it was also because they knew that this land bred people who, though they were far from being cultureless barbarians, obstinately adhered to their barbarism and had not lost touch with the primitive sources of being which they themselves had covered over with the mild rationalism of paganism.

Pain, which sensible pagans had trained themselves to treat with indifference both in themselves and other people, save when it could be used to add excitement to the public games, was here put to magic uses. Up till the conquest the Africans had worshipped Baal and Tanit, father and mother of fertility, who dispensed great gifts in return for human sacrifices; and this worship was afterwards continued under cover of the cult of Saturn, it is thought without complete mitigation of its harshness. In time the worshippers of Saturn moved almost in a body to the altars of Christianity; but this only brought back in another form this eerie talk of buying favours from the gods by suffering. Above this mob there appeared an army of magicians—prodigious in number, for it must not be forgotten that by far the larger part of Latin Christian literature was of African authorship—who spoke with terrible eloquence of various benefits, including immortality, procured by various sorts of deaths, including that of a god who had been crucified in an undignified sort of way, and those of quite base people who had been very properly executed by the State for refusal to obey the Imperial laws on such trifling matters as idolatry. Rome must have become familiar within her own doors with Christianity as a troubling secret society that gradually changed into something like a branch of the Civil Service; but from Africa and the East—and especially from Africa—must have come the knowledge of Christianity as a powerful threat to reason. Perhaps this accounts in part for Rome's disquieted awe of Africa; but, indeed, with the advent of Augustine came witness that their wildest stories of the land were true, for here was a lion that could understand language, a python whose coils could crush the upright Roman standard.

II

AUGUSTINE has himself told us the story of his first thirty-two years in his *Confessions,* with an unsurpassed truthfulness. He is one of the greatest of all writers, and he works in the same introspective field as the moderns. In his short, violent sentences, which constantly break out in the rudest tricks of the rhetoricians, rhymes, puns, and assonances, he tries to do exactly what Proust tries to do in his long, reflective sentences, which are so unconditioned by their words, which are so entirely determined by their meaning. He tries to take a cast of his mental state at a given moment. He will describe how it sometimes happened that when he went riding through the countryside he would see a dog coursing a hare in a field, and could not help being distracted from godly thought by the spectacle, not so much, he says, as 'to turn out of the road with the body of my horse, yet with the inclination of my heart,' although he knows well that this is a sport of the kind he has renounced the sight of in the public games. Not only is the experience itself depicted with the

15

clear colour and right form of master-painting, but a vast area of his temperament round the point of impact with this experience is illuminated also. One perceives the barbaric vitality which needed to be disciplined and acquainted with mildness, but which itself framed the discipline, so that in the end, though violence bent its neck to mildness, the proceedings were violent.

That no later novelist has surpassed him is proved by the frequency with which he reminds us of the immortal part of Tolstoy and transcends it. This is particularly true of two incidents in the *Confessions*. The first relates how a friend of his, an unbeliever as he himself was in those days, fell ill and was baptized by his family during a spell of unconsciousness. When Augustine visited him during his convalescence he jested with him concerning the baptism, and to his embarrassment and hidden anger was hotly rebuked for making a mock of sacred things. There has never been a better description of the change of temperature brought about in a friendship by a difference on an impersonal matter. The second relates how Alypius, his very mild and chaste friend, was haled by some companions to see the sword-players, sat with his eyes covered, uncovered them at the sound of a great cry from the people, saw blood, and from that moment was inflamed by a mad infatuation for the murderous sport. The passage is so Tolstoyan that one thinks of Alypius as a young Russian landowner. It does not flinch from recording that which is subtle and inexplicable on any rational basis; but there is no pretentious and perfunctory moral judgment attached to it. It is self-sufficient in its veracity as very little of Tolstoy is.

Nevertheless, we must not take the *Confessions* as altogether faithful to reality. It is too subjectively true to be objectively true. There are things in Augustine's life which he could not bear to think of at all, or very much, or without falsification, so the *Confessions* are not without gaps, understatements, and misstatements. And among these last may be counted the suggestions he makes against his father, Patricius. He speaks of him always in a tone of hatred and moral reprobation, which was probably quite unjustified. The worst he can say of the poor man is that he failed to exhort his son to chastity or the love of God, that he was ambitious for the worldly success of his son and looked forward eagerly to the time when he should marry and have children, and that he was hot-tempered. But male chastity, a virtue rarely found in vulgar profusion, was notoriously rare among Africans, and to expect such exhortations from any but a professed Christian was unreasonable; and Patricius did not abandon his paganism and submit to baptism till the end of his life. His ambitions for his son cannot be said to be disgraceful, in view of the fact that the Church bases its defence of the family partly on the supposition that the majority of fathers will lay just such hopeful plans for the perpetuity of their blood. And the accusation of hot temper shows a curious lack of generosity in Augustine, particularly when he has to make the grudging admission that this was counterbalanced by an unusual expansiveness of good will; for Patricius must have led a very troubled life.

He was a country gentleman of very narrow acres, and he belonged to the select but unlucky class of *curiales,* who were responsible for the taxes of their district. He must have known all the troubles which are suffered to-day by owners of agricultural land, and a great many more on top of those, due to the harsher provisions of the Roman tax system and the corruption of the administrative classes. If he was seized with frenzy a thousand times, there were probably nine hundred just occasions for it in

the caprice of the weather working on his
barren fields, the idleness of slaves, and the
exactions of tax-gatherers; and the remaining
hundred instances could be accounted for by
his marriage to a woman whose good temper
was of the sort that causes bad temper in
others. Augustine has left for us a vivid description of how it was Monnica's habit to tell
women who bore marks of their husbands'
blows on their disfigured faces that marriage
had made them their husbands' slaves, and
blame them for having rebelled against their
lawful masters. It is not probable that this
invariably represented a fair judgment on all
the matrimonial disputes of Thagaste, and in
any case it is not the kind of wisdom which
one would care to dispense to people who had
been recently subjected to physical pain. As if
in anticipation of the worst pedagogic affecta-
tions, this advice was given 'gravely, but with
a humorous air,' and was followed by a com-
placent boast that she herself was never beaten,
because she made it a rule never to contradict
her husband when he was angry, but would
wait her opportunity when he was calmer, and
would point out how unreasonable his conduct
had been. In fact, she was a smooth cliff of a
woman on whom the breakers of a man's virility

would dash in vain; and such order often causes its counterweight in disorder. Perhaps it would be unfair to expect Augustine to have seen this excuse for his father's choleric behaviour, since children rarely arrive at a just estimate of their parents' relationship. But it is strange that he should not have made some sympathetic allusion to his father's economic troubles, for they must have been brought home to him when he was fifteen, since he had then to be withdrawn from school, and would have had no further education had his father not made the most frantic efforts to collect some funds. It can only be explained by his love for his mother Monnica, which was so strong that he was bound to hate anyone who had a competing claim on her.

If a child looks at the superior force of its father and regards it not as so much protection but as the strength of the enemy against which it has to pit itself, the result is desperation, which may either paralyse it or move it to efforts so great as to be greatness. Plainly the process worked the latter way in Augustine's case; and there were other disharmonies in his surroundings which he took up as challenges to his will. It is probable that he had that feeling of uneasiness about his status which comes to children who are born to parents of

unequal rank. For Patricius belonged to the
landed classes, and his reluctance to abandon
paganism showed that he had affiliations with
the aristocracy; but Monnica's family had been
firm-rooted in Christianity for generations,
which suggests that they belonged to a lower
social level. It is quite certain that from both
sides alike he derived the embarrassment of
belonging to a conquered people racially different from their conquerors. Though Patricius was a landowner, he did not belong to one
of those Roman colonist families which were
as much the ascendant class as the Anglo-Irish
families used to be in Ireland; he was an
African like his wife. So Augustine was a
Numidian, a brother to the Berber and the
Tuareg, one of a people that are non-Semitic,
long of limb and sometimes fair-haired and
blue-eyed, but of bronze complexion and different mould from Europeans.

Augustine was, moreover, a poor provincial.
Thagaste lay in green and pleasant country,
among hills well wooded with pines and ilex
and watered by many streams. It gave him
the beautiful landscape of his mind's eye, on
which the artist in him constantly throws open
a window, even in those parts of his writings
which he most desired to be a blank cell of

abstract thought. But though it offered some share of urban delights in a theatre, a forum, and baths, the remains of these show that they were insignificant buildings. Thagaste was, in fact, only a free town of the second or third order, which owed its importance almost entirely to its site at the junction of several roads. He might, when he was older, go to Carthage; the prodigious rumour of that city must have been brought to him from earliest youth by the spectacle of the equipage and outriders of the Imperial Mail halted outside the inns of Thagaste. But he knew that even if he went to Carthage, even if he there became completely metropolitan, he would still be a provincial, because Africa was but a Roman colony. Only those could claim to be truly metropolitan who were citizens of Rome itself. Carthage was a marvellous city. Centuries ago it had been marvellous enough to excite the diabolical envy of Rome; it was the first of all cities to be built by plan, and the plan was stupendous. That pile of buildings which rose to the vast temple of the heathen god Eschmoun had long been effaced by war. For seventeen days the Romans kindled fires there till the home of seven hundred thousand people was a field of ashes, and they dragged the plough-

share about the vitrified ruins. But so potent
were the forces which had worked to engender
a city at this spot, that after destruction it
rose again, second in area and population only
to Rome, and the equal of Alexandria. The
temple of Eschmoun was now dedicated to
Aesculapius, but the same beauty and luxury
and African might informed the town. One
may know how gorgeous a city Carthage was
in Augustine's time from the circumstance that,
centuries later, after successive invaders had
looted her again and again, the best of Tunis
and Pisa was built from her marble residue.
But for all that, Carthage was not Rome. It
was an African city.

In that lay the secret of its power to be re-
born after ruin; and Augustine, who must
have felt his own genius as characteristically
African, must have known this well. But the
Romans, being conquerors, had imposed a
standard of values which set their values above
African values. When the Africans bent Latin
to their own purposes, it was taken for granted
that they were spoiling it, though they had
done nothing more than develop the archaic
forms which had been brought over to them
centuries before by their conquerors, and the
Romans had done exactly the same thing to

make their contemporary Latin. Whenever
African and Roman practice differed, it was
taken for granted that the Africans were wrong;
and, unhappily, in a sense this assumption was
warranted. To Rome, the centre of the world,
hastened all the most skilled artists and artifi-
cers, philosophers and rhetoricians. These, by
mingling with each other, and by listening to
the criticism of their patrons, who had been
educated to expertness by their opportunities
for appreciation, could raise their manners and
their work to a pitch of accomplishment which
could hardly be conceived elsewhere. At the
thought of that polished and clannish society
any provincial would feel himself clumsy and
isolated, even if he knew that he had power
within him such as none of these metropolitans
could possibly claim. Such was the case of
Augustine, and in this matter he reminds us
again of Tolstoy. Each alike lived with barbarism at his back, on the fringe of a civilisation
which stood to him for a refinement and self-
possession which he at once hated and envied;
and each was ashamed of his envy, because of
his consciousness that the crude strength he
drew from his barbaric soil was worth infinitely
more than any refinement and self-possession.

So life laid down a certain number of challenges to Augustine. He was the son of an overpowering and resented father, he was born of an unequal marriage, he was one of a subject people, he was a provincial, and no migration to Carthage could save him from a still superior metropolitan scorn. Of all these challenges he must have been acutely aware; he had such an inflamed pride that when he was forty-six years old he could write with a blistering pen of how his elders had teased him about the punishments he underwent at school. And all these challenges he could have accepted, as ultimately he did, but the issues were not then clear. They were all associated with his father, or at least the male side of life. But there was also his mother. We know nothing of Monnica save what her son tells us, and that is plainly often a distortion of reality. The fact of her Christianity throws very little light on her character, any more than the fact of Protestantism would tell us much about a woman born in England during the century after the Reformation. It was a natural form of religion for one in her position. What we learn beyond all reasonable doubt is that she was an energetic woman full of good sense and worldly wisdom, whose outstanding virtue was a certain steady self-control which her son, because he himself and his father so conspicuously lacked it, very greatly admired. She was a haven of calm to him, and she was willing to be that for ever. She did not want her son to grow up. Once, over his wine, Patricius told her that he had been watching the boy at the baths and had seen such signs of manhood that they might hope to have grandchildren about them before long. This happened after Patricius had become a Christian catechumen, so it is highly unlikely that he meant anything indecorous, anything other than that desire for heirs which the landowner, bless his optimistic soul, does not lose in the worst of times. But Monnica fell into a shuddering alarm.

It was fortunate that in her religion she had a perfect and, indeed, noble instrument for obtaining her desire that her son should not become a man. Very evidently Christianity need not mean emasculation, but the long struggles of Augustine and Monnica imply that in his case it did. Monnica could have put him into the Church as into a cradle. He would then take vows of continence and annul the puberty she detested. He would worship the eternal power of the Trinity and never use his will in the polity that man has set up for the exercise of temporal power. To him the sword would not be a weapon to which he stretched out his hand, but one to which he bowed his neck, and a son dead is as much a mother's undisputed property as a son not yet born; and she could bear to contemplate this death since it would only happen in fantasy, would only be enacted in the emotional attitude of the Church now that the assaults of Julian the Apostate had failed and Christianity was firmly established. With her smooth competence she must have been able to make the Church a most alluring prospect for one who, with his dislike of his father, and his addiction to unsparing self-criticism, must have hated violence almost as urgently as his pride recommended it to him.

Thus two alternatives faced Augustine. Would he keep to the world of men, and in the field of action or pagan letters become such a great man that his father looked little beside him, that it would become apparent there was no base alloy in him and a subject race could produce masters, that Carthage would forget he was a squireen's son and Rome forget he was an African? Or would he turn his back on the world of men and pass into another world which denied the standard of values held by Patricius, Carthage, Rome, and presented him with another standard that, if he accepted it, would raise him at one step above the greatest man in Rome, would utterly contemn the accomplishments of civilisation, and indeed reward him for lacking them, and what was more, would ensure him pre-eminence in the future life as well as in this? The decision was not easy to make, for it was a choice between violence and control, between discord and harmony, between heat and light, and he was torn between love and hate of all these things. History, moreover, was disturbing the simplicity of the alternatives. The Roman Empire had been so mighty that the mere fact of its failure could not displace the legend of its supreme power; the gospel story and the blood of the martyrs had fixed the character of the Christian Church as meek. Yet if one had a disposition to seek the quiet of death, not by immediate flight out of life but by association with dying things, one might find gratification in the service of the Empire; and when the Church was made official and began to exert power in secular affairs it exchanged the coolness of resignation to the tomb for the liveliness and sweat of action. In the conflict that was waged on the battlefield of Augustine's soul there was a great confusion of enemies and allies. Even Monnica could not give him a whole-hearted summons to her side. She could not bear him to assume adult status even in the Church. Hence, though at his birth he was signed with the cross and touched on his tongue with the symbolic salt, she did not insist on his baptism, for reasons which one so conversant with Church custom must have known to be specious. It was the custom among the lax to delay baptism as long as possible, so that as many sins as possible should be annulled by the holy waters and anointment; but Monnica, who prided herself on her orthodoxy, must have been aware that the strictest opinion in the Church favoured infant baptism.

III

THE boy hated school. The chief cause of his resentment against it was certainly the humiliation it inflicted on his infant dignity; and he had that precocious insight into character which is as sand in the engine of any educational machine. In a curiously petulant and extremely Tolstoyan complaint against the discipline applied to children to make them acquire learning which will probably only lead them into intellectual folly when they are older, he points out that 'my master, if in any trifling question he were foiled by another schoolmaster, was presently more racked with choler and envy at him, than I was, when at a match at tennis-ball, I lost my game to my play-fellow.' Human nature being what it is, it usually goes ill with children who notice things like these. It is also possible that he annoyed his masters still further by apparent stupidity, for a literary mind like Augustine's is apt in childhood to flee from drudgery into reverie, and his loathing recapitulation of the chant, 'One and one make two, two and two make four,' shows what sort of subject he found most difficult. In any case, his natural incapacities were bound to be increased by the alien character of the school work, which was designed for the Romanisation of African children. The native culture had been suppressed, and all that education could do was to aim at the exploitation of such talents as the pupils possessed for the benefit of the Roman system; so it offered just the same combination of material inducements and exasperations to the racial genius as the educational system devised by the British for India.

At first Augustine was in school at Thagaste; but later, when he was fourteen, he was sent to study at a much more important town between twenty and thirty miles away, called Madaura, which is now Mdaourouch in Algeria. It was a stimulating place for a boy with literary talents, as it was the Stratford-on-Avon of Africa. Apuleius had been born there two centuries before. Of all African writers he is the best known to us to-day, because Walter Pater inserted in *Marius the Epicurean* a translation of the delicious story of Cupid and Psyche from *The Golden Ass,* and made Apuleius himself one of his characters; and he symbolised literature in the popular mind of his land just as Shakespeare symbolised it for ours. He was the centre of a national cult. This was not only because of his rich imagination, which enabled him to write the first and probably the finest picaresque novel ever written, and to inseminate the later geniuses of Boccaccio and Cervantes and Le Sage, nor because of his romantic style, which firmly resisted the standardising and rationalising influence of Roman literature and asserted the varied forms and colours of life. It was chiefly because he dealt so often with magic, an approach to the secrets of the universe very dear to the African mind, which, having kept its primitive vigour, constantly created symbols which are next door to spells. Everything Numidian in Augustine must have answered to Apuleius' appeal, and his ambition must have longed for like fame. But all the Christian in him must have recoiled, not because the Church disbelieved in magic, but because it believed in it and feared it. The special reason it forbade Christians to take part in the worship of the gods was that it believed the gods to be demons, and the ceremonies of their service to be magical practice. Apuleius, to devout Christians such as Monnica, must have been a doorkeeper of Hell.

But during boyhood the Christian influence had not much power over Augustine. He himself says that this period was full of abnormal depravity, particularly during his sixteenth year, which he had to spend at home, as his family could no longer afford his school fees. But it is quite possible that this is a distortion of fact due to the excessive development in him of the sense of guilt, which we all have, and which seems to be due rather to an inherent shame of the human being at its common experiences than to acquired shame at individual experiences. Certainly he confesses to homosexual relationships in a sentence which, with characteristic insight, puts its finger on the real offence of homosexuality, by pointing out that it brings the confusion of passion into the domain where one ought to be able to practise calmly the art of friendship. No doubt there was a time when he was a horried little boy, but there have been a lot of horrid little boys since the world began. The only other sample of his iniquity he gives us is a raid which he and some friends made on a neighbour's pear tree, which he describes in a passage that takes one's breath away by its penetrating analysis of the gratuitous character of adolescent delinquency. He and his friends did not want the pears. They picked far more than they could eat, and threw them to the hogs. It was simply a demonstration against order, the cherished work of the adult; in fact, it was an *acte gratuit* of the sort that fills M. André Gide with such ecstasy. But it is very unlikely that Augustine, if he had really had a past of unexampled viciousness, would have cited such a commonplace piece of schoolboy mischief.

Whatever that side of his life may have been, it did not interfere with his intellectual growth. His literary interests continued, before and after his father had scraped together enough money to send him to the schools at Carthage. He must have been debarred from much pleasure that would normally have come his way during training as a rhetorician by his dislike of Greek. Though he forced himself to acquire some knowledge of it, his natural hatred of suavity inclined his heart against it. But from boyhood he greatly enjoyed the poetry of Virgil, and loved to bewail with proper feeling the exile of Aeneas and the death of Dido, and to put forth new versions of the lament of Juno on the departure into Italy of the Trojan king. By such studies he acquired a mastery of language that won him a high place in the Rhetoric Schools of Carthage; and we hear of him being crowned in a poetical competition. The intellectual and artistic activity that seethed round him there, particularly in the theatres, excited him greatly.

All went very well with him. Presently his father died; it shows how much Augustine had disliked him that, though he was particularly sensitive to the tragedy of death, he chronicles the event with complete indifference, and only mentions it to explain why his allowance was coming to him from his mother. He had set his sexual life in order. At first he had been promiscuous, though not from entirely sensual motives; he says that he delighted— and from the form taken by his religious devotions we know this to be true—in the emotions of loving and being loved. There was an obvious way out of this situation. He himself expresses wonder and resentment that his parents had not arranged for his marriage at the early age which was customary in Africa. But although Patricius had been willing to do this, Monnica had not. She had pleaded that an unsuitable marriage might give him a 'she-clog' on his ambitions. But Augustine settled the matter in his own way by falling in love with a woman to whom he joined himself in a bond of fidelity that was virtually marriage. There was probably some valid reason why he did not marry her; she may have been a manumitted slave, in which case her marriage to a man of superior class was forbidden by Roman law, but she would not be despised by society if she entered into concubinage with him.

However that may have been, the union was so happy that it became permanent, and Augustine avows that he was strictly faithful. He records this relationship in a passage which is puzzling enough read by itself. 'In those days I kept a mistress not joined to me in lawful marriage; but one found out by wandering lust empty of understanding; yet had I but that one, towards whom I truly kept the promise of the bed; in whom I might by mine own example learn experience, what difference there would be betwixt the knot of the marriage covenant, mutually consented unto for the desire of children, and the bargain of a lustful love, where though children be against our wills begotten, yet being born they even compel us to love them.' This means nothing at all save that their bodily relations had been happy, for when he wrote this passage in his *Confessions* he had come to believe that sexual pleasure was a deadly shame. Later still, in *The City of God,* he was to indulge in wistful speculations, so naïve and so detailed that a fairly robust translator leaves them in what Gibbon called 'the decent obscurity of a learned language,' as to the manner in which the business of propagation might have been conducted had not man fallen and been under the disgraceful necessity of soiling himself with enjoyment. For there was to grow in him to morbid proportions as he grew older that unhappy attitude to sex, consisting of an exaggerated sense of its importance combined with an unreasoning horror of it, which is not uncommon among men but rare among women other than those affected with hysteria. The cause of this attitude may lie to some extent in the less dignified anatomy of man, a point on which Augustine copiously complained; but it may lie to some extent in the disadvantageous situation of man in the sexual act, who finds that for him it ends with physical collapse and the surrender of power, whereas for his partner it ends with motherhood and an increase of power. In any case, this tendency had not yet developed in Augustine, and he was happy enough to call the child that compelled his love Adeodatus, 'given by God.' It is true that it is not safe to draw too definite conclusions from this name, because it was the custom in Christian Africa, as in Puritan England and America, to attach to children such pious labels as Born-in-grace, As-God-wills-it, Praise-God, and God-be-with-him. Yet even though that custom existed, Augustine, to whom words meant much, to whom talk of God meant more, would hardly have called his child by that name if his mind had not been at rest in his family. The name of the child's mother we do not know. Both she and the young man whose death Augustine lamented in chapters which are the supreme analysis of grieving friendship in all literature, slink nameless through his pages. It is as if he felt that they had no right to be there, that there should have been no one in his heart except Monnica.

But in spite of Augustine's immense gifts and early promise, and in spite of the order he had imposed on his personal life, he did not succeed as a rhetorician. Slowly the shadow of failure passes over the pages of the *Confessions*. He can hardly bear to write of it; but he preserves the mournful dignity of a sick lion, and is nobly unembittered, speaking no jealous word against his successful rivals. It is true that he had always a following of admiring friends, but these were not eminent nor even always very discerning young men. Certainly he produced no work except a treatise on the Beautiful and the Good, which attracted no attention whatsoever, and seemed the most unlikely candidate for fame. This impotence of his genius can only be explained by the fatality that his vocation was obviously for imaginative writing and that he had renounced the use of the imagination. His hostile attitude to art, which is dogmatically expressed in several places in his work, has very deep roots. It is, of course, not uncommon. Art is bound to come under the censorship of our sense of guilt, which suspects all our activities if they are not part of processes that we hope will redeem us from our stains, not by giving pleasure but by withholding it; and it is bound to incur the disapproval of the death-wish we all have in varying degrees, since by analysing experience it makes us able to handle experience and increase our hold on life. But Augustine's hostility to art was given a special vigour, because it proceeded not only from these causes but from the political situation which had such a dynamic effect on him.

Augustine's case falls under a few headings. He examines the poetry of Virgil, and declares it absurd that he should have been taught to lament the death of Dido when he was still indifferent to his own spiritual death, 'caused by not loving Thee, O God, light of my heart and bread of the inner mouth of my soul.' He objects to the stories of the gods, because they frequently represent them as engaged in lecheries and crimes which the people are tempted to imitate because they hear them recounted with praise and admiration. And he objects to stage plays, because they arouse in the audience factitious emotion of a hysterical and unprofitable sort. Now, this must remind us at once of Tolstoy's *What is Art?* which makes exactly the same points. It is true that Augustine's case against art is more logically put than Tolstoy's, shows greater cultivation, and is devoid of many of his absurdities. It would never have occurred to Augustine to lay it down that society, having organised herself so badly that a section of her population is illiterate and inexperienced, should limit the functions of her highest faculty to the understanding of that section, disregarding the fact that only by the unfettered exercise of those functions can she discover the faults in herself which lead her into bad organisation; and his denigration of pagan activities never took such an idiotic form as Tolstoy's proud citation of the comminatory remarks passed by his daughter, 'a gifted art student,' on the works of Renoir, Manet, Monet,

Redon, and Pissaro. But Tolstoy comes very close to Augustine when he complains that all works of art which arouse other feelings than love of God and brotherliness towards men are deflecting our forces from another end; that when people are rewarded by fame and wealth for the power to create beauty through music or painting or literature, this is discouraging to children and peasants, who only admire people for being very strong or very good; and to create an artistic illusion, as in Wagner's operas, is to switch the audience into a world of nonsense.

Each of them is a man living on the fringe of a great civilisation which, by conquering or ignoring the culture of his native land, has imposed its culture on him. Consequently it forces him and his people to apply its standards to their art; but as no people can create according to any standards other than those they find in their own breast, this means that they are prevented from full artistic achievement. But the affected people will not complain of this grievance, since that would amount to confessing that they have been conquered, and that the conquerors have really succeeded in doing them harm. So they try to annul the whole question by wiping out art. They declare that art is reprehensible unless it has an explicit religious and moral content; and as this is just what authentic art never has—since its business is to press ahead and discover the yet unformulated truths which can afterwards be formulated in terms of religion and morals—they therefore wipe out all the superior artistic achievement of the conquerors. It may be beautiful, but it is not good. So the conquered lift themselves to a level with their conquerors, or are possibly even above them; and even individuals whose gifts could triumph over any limitations are forced to adopt this attitude because of their smarting national consciousness.

This was the process that robbed Africa of a name which should have ranked higher than Apuleius, and Latin literature of a name that might have ranked with Virgil, and that made Augustine the instrument of the Catholic Church, and the Catholic Church the instrument of Augustine. He never essayed the imaginative work for which he had such an unsurpassed endowment; and he found sanction for the surrender in a pagan book, Cicero's *Hortensius*. This is now lost, but we can judge its quality from certain quoted passages. It seems to have been bland rather than stimulating, and perhaps its appeal to Augustine lay in its confirmation of the wisdom of his flight from the more artistic opportunities of a rhetorician's life. 'In the next world,' it asked, 'what need will there be of eloquence? *There* no legal processes will be needed. There our blessedness will consist in the study of virtue and the advance of knowledge. Other objects of endeavour are matters of necessity; this only is a matter of delight.' The book filled him with a desire to be a philosopher, so ardent that one wonders why, in a being whose ardour must have had such a compelling quality, it did not procure him success. But he had not, perhaps, the perfect equipment for a philosopher. He was under the practical disadvantage of being unable to keep discipline among his pupils; and he lacked many of the intellectual qualifications for philosophic discussion. Only once—when he had a story to tell, in his *Confessions*—did he show any sense of form; and that can only be said if one lops off the philosophical chapters at the end. Nearly all his religious treatises are integrated by religious fervour rather than by any recognition that a work should have a beginning, a middle, and an end. He was, moreover, apt to grow passionate, personal, and careless of logic in argument. But not only was he unrewarded by success in philosophy, it brought him no more inner peace. The book *Hortensius* could not satisfy him, since nowhere was there written in it the name of Christ, for which he listened always, like a child waiting for its mother's voice to call it in from its play to feed and rest. Feeling that lack, he laid the book aside and turned to the Holy Scriptures; but he was repelled by the contrast between the ruggedness of the old Latin version and the Ciceronian pomp, the pagan polish which he envied and loathed and admired more than anything else in the world. It was then that he was seized upon by a force which introduced a new element into his life, which had nothing to do with Patricius or Monnica, which was of neither Rome nor Africa, which came out of Asia. He became a Manichæan.

We know little enough of Manichæanism, for it rose as a rival to the Church just at the time when Constantine made Christianity the State religion and the bishops and magistrates joined to destroy the heretical writings. Hence we are forced to derive our knowledge of its doctrines and origins chiefly from accounts of its opponents, but what we know is enough to show us that it was not so much a religion as a work of art. The founder was a Persian called Mani, who was born about a hundred

and forty years before Augustine, in 215 A.D.
Tradition describes him as wearing the dress
of a Persian sage, and we can well imagine him
with a mantle of changeable blue taffeta, one
green shoe and one red, an ebony staff in the
right hand, and a book of mysteries under the
left arm; for through the ages we suspect something fantastic and bedizened about his genius.
But tradition also tells us that he was a great
painter, and won fame both by decorating tem-
ples and illuminating manuscripts; and that too
we can believe, for every shred of knowledge we
have about his work tells us that here was a man
so immersed in the artistic process that he knew
no other. The myth he created has grandeur
and profundity. Light and darkness, good and
evil, are the same pair under different names.
Some might say that the pair is also known
under the name of matter and spirit, but it is
doubtful if Mani ever advanced so far in the
way of abstract thought as the conception of
matter. Being an artist, he worked with the
concrete, and gave the kingdom of light a personal ruler who was God, and put the kingdom
of darkness under the lordship of Satan and his
angels.

For long the two kingdoms were unaware of
each other. Then Satan made war on the king-

dom of light, and God begat Primal Man on His consort to be His champion and defender. But Primal Man was vanquished and thrown into captivity. God Himself then took the field, routed evil, and released the captive. But meanwhile there had been wrought a malicious and not easily reparable confusion of the two kingdoms. Seeds of darkness had been scattered widely in the soil of light, innumerable seeds of light found themselves sown deeply in the darkness. These elements must be sorted and returned to their own. For this purpose the universe was created. It is planned as a means of deliverance for the stolen particles of light. In the sun dwells Primal Man, and in the moon dwells Primal Woman, and the signs of the Zodiac, like dredging buckets on a revolving wheel, raise the rescued particles to be cared for by these two and returned after purification to their proper kingdom. On earth man plays out a peculiar drama of division. He is the work of Satan, who placed in his dark substance all the particles of light he could steal, so that he could control them. Man is, therefore, a house divided against itself. Demons seek to aid the darkness in him by preaching him false religions, of which Judaism is the worst; and certain activities, notably the eating

46

of flesh, the taking of life, and sexual darkness, cause dark victories. The light in him is enfranchised by the teaching of the true prophets, Adam, Noah, Abraham, Zoroaster, Buddha, the phantom Christ who made use of the Messiah of the Jews, who was really a demon, Paul, and Mani himself. When all the particles of light are liberated the kingdom of light will be perfected, the good angels who maintain the present universe will withdraw the prop of their power from it, and it will collapse into fiery nothingness. The kingdom of darkness will not be annulled. It is a part of reality. But the kingdoms will be distinct and separate.

It is a beautiful myth, and how nearly it corresponds to a basic fantasy of the human mind is shown by its tendency to reappear spontaneously in age after age. Moreover, it has the practical advantage of presenting the ordinary human being with a hypothesis which explains the extraordinary and unpleasant things which are constantly happening to him externally and internally and suggest that all is going as well as can be expected. It is not surprising that Augustine remained under its spell for nine years, particularly as it gave him the opportunity to take back art into his life under the title of religion. But it must be admitted that there is a profound mystery about his adherence to Manichæanism, for his later attacks on it show very imperfect knowledge of its doctrine, and are even tainted with that vulgarity and crudity which one finds in attacks on creeds made by people whose knowledge of those creeds has been acquired only for the purpose of attack. These inconsistencies can only be explained by supposing that, as so often happens to very gifted people in their youth, he passed through a period of moonish reverie, during which he thought a great deal of Manichæanism but not very alertly, and attended at their services regularly but did not listen very vigilantly. Certainly the fundamental elements of Manichæanism sank into him; to them he owed the recognition of dualism as a source of distress which he imported into Christianity. Certainly also he converted several friends to it, and professed it with sufficient vehemence to defy the disapproval of Monnica, who forbade him her house when he returned to Thagaste.

This appears a curiously harsh action, for the incident occurred at the very beginning of his adherence to Manichæanism, when he was an exceedingly young man; and, as she herself reveals in an anecdote, it was contrary to the advice given by the Church to the relatives of infidels. But there was probably a sufficiently poignant cause for Monnica's distress. She had been left by her husband in straitened circumstances, and she must have found the necessity to maintain her son and his concubine and child a heavy burden; and meanwhile her position in the Church must have improved. Widows who had taken vows of celibacy were granted special privileges by the Church, as if they were being rewarded for a triumph over the turbulent quality of maleness. There is something very sinister about the emphasis with which they are exhorted to dignity and sobriety; so might mutes be bidden to behave when returning from the successful accomplishment of an interment. In its mixture of material and spiritual exasperations her situation might possibly be compared to that of a necessitous lady, well known for her piety and good works in Anglican circles, with a son for whom she could easily get an excellent living if he would only be ordained, but who insists on being an unsuccessful journalist and an enthusiastic Theosophist. In any case, we cannot accuse her of harshness, only of a harsh intention, which broke down under the comfort she adminis-

tered herself as human beings were able to do
in those days when dreams were believed to be
divine communications. It seemed to her in
her sleep that she was standing weeping on a
wooden rule and was approached by a radiant
young man who enquired the cause of her sadness. She explained that she was weeping because of her son's Manichæanism, and he bade
her look about her and see that where she was
there was Augustine also; and when she turned
about, there he was, standing beside her on the
rule. So she took this as proof that he would
return to grace, and she admitted him again to
her table and her fireside. When she told him
her reason for relenting, he pointed out that the
dream might have another interpretation: it
might mean that she would become a Manichæan. But she answered, 'No, it was not told
me, thou art where he is, but where thou art,
there he is.' With Augustine's genius for recording subtleties, he notes that what struck
him most was not his mother's dream, even with
its suggestion of supernatural intervention in
his affairs, but the characteristic cool shrewd-
ness of this answer. It rings through the Latin
to-day, his adoring recognition of Monnica's essential quality: what she wanted fitted in with
what was, as neatly as if she were playing cup-

and-ball. Such a woman could afford to wait. The son of such a woman could afford to wander, knowing he would be brought home at last.

IV

So for nine years Augustine wandered in his only half-attentive preoccupation with Manichæanism. Then he began to weary. This faith was a work of art; so he renounced it, partly because of his hostility to art, partly because in fact no work of art can take the place of a religion. A work of art is the analysis of an experience, an expression of the consciousness of the universe at a particular moment. Religion aims at the analysis of all experience, at an expression of the consciousness of the universe through all time. It claims through revelation and prayer to arrive at the final knowledge which art can conceive of existing only at the inconceivable moment when all works of art have been created. Augustine became aware that Mani could not make this claim. He was an artist, and a romantic artist at that. Digging in his mind with the purpose of formulating yet unformulated truths, he brought up the false with the true, the trivial with the weighty, the superficial fancy that masks the deep fantasy. For a time Augustine tried to allay his doubts by working under a certain Manichæan bishop named Faustus, but he was left unsatisfied. He is careful to state that this was not because Faustus had a beautiful faculty of eloquence; one realises how long the 'plain blunt man' has been about his horrid work when one finds Augustine protesting that 'nothing is true because roughly delivered, nor false because graced in the speaking.' He was dissatisfied because he found Faustus a poor scholar, unable to explain the discrepancies between the philosophers' and the Manichæans' views on natural science, and not very interested in them. He seemed to have no appetite for finality, he was content to work on half-apprehended hints, the symbols used by others set working in him his own imaginative set of symbols and not an imperative desire for understanding. In fact, he was an artist as Augustine was, and as Augustine longed not to be. So Augustine detached his heart from Manichæanism, and in a burning sentence compressed his case against its teasing artistic quality, its substitution of Jesus who was a phantom for the Very Son of God: 'These were the dishes wherein to me, hunger-starven for Thee, they served up the sun and moon.'

But Augustine did not make his way straight

to the Church. He knew he could afford to wander a little longer. He decided to go to Rome. Friends had promised him there a position of better pay and greater dignity, among more disciplined students. So, with his concubine and his son, he set sail for Ostia in his thirtieth year. This step was passionately opposed by Monnica, who travelled from Thagaste to beg him not to go. He was able to get on board the ship only by telling her that he had a friend whom he had to see off on a voyage, and by bidding her wait for him in an oratory erected to St. Cyprian, close by the harbour; and on discovering his deception she fell into an agony of sorrow. Perhaps because of this, he did not feel happy on his travels. For Rome in her pride, the ruins of which strike us with amazement, he has not one word of praise. He knew there the misery of a proud provincial who cannot compel the metropolis to recognise his powers, and a sickness, probably malaria, overcame him. His friends, who included the mild Alypius, now an assessor in the Italian Bounty office, helped him to find pupils; but Roman students, though orderly, had a mean habit of not paying. Worst of all, in his search for belief he had come on a blank wall. He fell for a little time under the influence of the Sceptical philosophers, who held that we can know nothing about the nature of things, and therefore should withhold judgment on all fundamental problems and cultivate imperturbability. But this was not a philosophy that could satisfy a man with a mind like a fountain of enquiry; as well might a lion resolve on vegetarianism. He abandoned this line of thought as soon as he received his first summons to greatness, which, oddly enough, resulted from a visit paid by Symmachus, the pagan Prefect of Rome, to the young Emperor Valentinian and his mother Justina at the Imperial Court at Milan, for the purpose of explaining why the Senate had rebuilt an altar to Victory which had been dismantled out of respect for the Christian religion. For the Milanese had asked Symmachus, who was a well-known amateur of letters, to send them from Rome a good professor of rhetoric; and Augustine was recommended to him by some Manichæan friends.

This was Augustine's first success since his student days, and it was considerable, for though Milan was smaller than Rome, it had the prestige attaching to the Imperial residence. It had an enormous effect on him, because it brought him under the spell of Bishop Ambrose. Augustine was bound to become infatuated with this man, because he was everything that Augustine was not, and pretended to hate, and longed to be. Ambrose was an aristocrat, the son of a prefect, who had himself been a lawyer, a magistrate, and the Governor of Liguria before he was chosen, much against his wishes and in spite of the fact that he was not yet baptized, bishop of the most important see in North Italy. He was a superb human being, a princely leader, a successful negotiator, a fluent preacher, a notably fine Greek scholar. Augustine could not take his eyes off him. He listened to all his sermons in the basilica, he called on him constantly at his home. But it is obvious that Ambrose felt no reciprocal emotion towards the new professor of rhetoric, this awkward Numidian, who had come on the recommendation of his enemy Symmachus (whom he had neatly worsted in this matter of the restored altar) and was understood to have Manichæan associations. One might as well expect an Archbishop of York to receive with open arms a young Maori who had been appointed to an educational post in York on the recommendation of some well-known Secularist such as Mr. J. M. Robertson, and who showed sympathies with Theosophy.

The resultant relationship is the subject of a passage in the *Confessions* which is a masterpiece of honest and subtle observation, and a most amusing example of the triumph of repressed feeling. 'As for Ambrose himself, I esteemed him a very happy man according to the world, whom personages of such authority so much honoured; only his remaining a bachelor seemed a painful course unto me.' In that phrase rings an implied criticism, a covert pride. The other man gets worldly success, but if he had real power, of which virility is the symbol, could he bear to be celibate, as I cannot bear to be? But Augustine goes on to explain that he knows nothing of 'what hopes he carried about him, what strugglings he felt against the temptations his very eminence was subject to,' for when Augustine went to see him he was either engaged with many people, or was refreshing 'his body with necessary sustenance, or his mind with reading.' There was no trouble about seeing him. Anybody could go into his room; but nobody was announced, and he ignored everybody. Simply he went on reading. He did not even read aloud, perhaps because he feared lest his audience should break in with demands for an exposition, or perhaps because he was husbanding his voice; 'with what intent soever he did it,' says Augustine loyally, 'that man certainly had a good meaning in it.' There

was nothing for his visitors to do save go away.
One perceives clearly under the surface of Augustine's prose what he was thinking as he sat
in the quiet room and looked at the prince of
the Church, so reasonably and yet so insolently
turning over the pages of his books and withdrawing into his superb self. He was rightly
supposing that posterity would see Ambrose
not as the prince of the Church who in self-
protection had turned a blank face on the tire-
some provincial, but as a prince of the Church
who lost his opportunity to speak like an equal
with a king of the Church. But the lion knows
only a blunt and honourable form of malice.
His honesty, his delicate discrimination, made
him continue to realise that this man was a
marvel of precious distinction.

So the influence of Ambrose continued to
work on him, powerfully as if he were his
father, but without arousing resistance, as if
he were a father so gentle that no son could
feel him as a challenge. Ambrose's sermons
must have pleased the demand of the artist in
Augustine for suavity by their fine Italian Latin
and gracious style; and presently the ordered
thought behind them began to resolve his deep
and troublesome perplexities. It happened
that Ambrose was greatly given to subjecting

the Scriptures to allegorical interpretation, a method of exegesis which the Greek theologians had borrowed from the cultured pagans, who had long used it to excuse the cantrips of the immortals, and thus he was able to smooth away Augustine's disgust at the barbarism of the Old Testament. He also smoothed away Augustine's objection to authority, and made him agree comfortably that, just as he was able to accept the fact that he was the son of Patricius and Monnica though he had no first-hand knowledge of it, even so might he be able to take other truths at second-hand. Moreover, Ambrose was able to insinuate into Augustine's mind, past his marked preference for the concrete, the conception of a spiritual substance; hitherto one of his chief difficulties in accepting the Christian God had been that he could not see how He could exist without being corporal. So complete was the victory of Ambrose's suavity that when Monnica came to her son from Africa, as she did about a year after his establishment in Milan, he was able to tell her that he had become a Christian catechumen, and was only waiting for some direct mark of the divine will to be baptized. One can see how keen and new his enjoyment of gentleness was, and how alien from his violent and senseless temper, by his wonder at Monnica's cheerful obedience when she was forbidden by the sexton at a Milanese shrine to practise her country custom of offering her fellow-worshippers bites and sups from a little basket containing wine and cheese-cakes, so as to make a little feast of remembrance. The custom had been forbidden by the Bishop because it had led to disorderly picnicking. Augustine apparently would have thought it natural if she had made some rebellious scene, and, linking the two who had opened to him the springs of mildness, he happily wondered whether she would have resigned herself so easily to the breaking of her country custom had it not been enjoined by marvellous Ambrose.

But he would not go at once into the fold. He would take his own time. He was a lion, not a lamb. He and his friend Alypius, who had followed him from Rome, and Nebridius, a young man whose infatuation for Augustine had made him leave his home in Africa simply to be with him, gathered together in a gentle and rather amateurish little company of truth-seekers. They read—or rather Augustine read and expounded to the others—the works of the Neoplatonic philosophers. It throws a curious light on Augustine's equipment for his career

that he had not yet read them, and that he had
to read the *Enneads* of Plotinus in the Latin
translation of Victorinus. Naturally they were
enchanted by that delectable philosopher, who
has sustained so many of the finest human beings even to our own day. He offered them
a philosophy which was very near to a religion,
which was, indeed, very near to being Christianity, since from its foundations it had constantly
borrowed from Christian thought and repaid its
loans by influencing Christian thinkers. Many
Christians, such as Origen and Eusebius and
Athanasius and Hilary of Poictiers and Ambrose
himself, had been deeply influenced by Neo-
platonism, which put before them ideas hardly
at all alien from the Christian faith. It held
that the first duty of human beings is to seek
the knowledge of God; that God is a Trinity;
that evil is nothing but nihilism, a patch in the
matter which is the dark substratum of the universe accidentally uninvaded by God; that we
can only come to the knowledge of God by
chastity and temperance of body and mind, and
by the practice of contemplation in degrees of
increasing intensity, rising to mystical ecstasy.
It was a system of thought as elevated as Christianity, but lacking in the one element that
would bind Augustine's soul.

What that was one may see if one contrasts the Neoplatonic and the Christian Trinity. The first person of the Neoplatonic Trinity was pure Existence, Goodness, or Unity, present everywhere in the finite world, yet infinite, the supreme reality on which all other things depend. From this proceeds Universal Mind, which only knows the world of ideas, of abstract thought; it knows nothing of the material world and plays no providential part in the affairs of man. From this proceeds the World-Soul, which is immaterial like Mind, but stands between Mind and the material world, and has elected to confuse itself with the world of phenomena; it creates souls of various kinds, including those of men, which are capable of rising to union with it or sinking into matter. In this Trinity the First Person has no knowledge of the Second or Third persons, being superior to thought; and the Second Person has no knowledge of the Third. No love is felt by a superior for an inferior, only by inferiors for their superiors. This is entirely different from the gracious conception of the Christian Trinity, which lives in loving, reciprocal relations and cultivates a common aim in the redemption of mankind. Above all, it lacks the figure of Christ. 'No man in these books,'

writes Augustine at the end of a burning chapter, 'hears him calling, Come unto me, all ye
that labour.'

This delicate Neoplatonism had no real
chance of holding Augustine, whose most
severely abstract thought is damp with his sweat.
But it enchanted the three Carthaginians with
its grace, its polish, its manifest 'superiority,'
and they wished that they too could be philosophers and spend their days in the pursuit of
wisdom. But how was it to be done? Augustine was still not meeting with the worldly success for which he hoped. There is a pathetic
chapter, which leaves the very taste of failure
in the mouth, describing how he paced the
streets of Milan, trying to grind out a syco-
phantic oration in praise of the Emperor, and
saw a drunken beggar, and wished he could
change places with him. One feels sure that
that oration was not a success. Augustine must
have been one of those innately, indeed invol-
untarily, sincere people whose sincerity is never
more glaringly apparent than when they try
to be insincere. For this reason, and others,
he could only make a living by toil so con-
tinuous that it left him no leisure for thought.
The mornings were taken up by teaching, and
the rest of the day had to be spent keeping up

influential connections and writing discourses for sale to his scholars. Alypius and Nebridius could not offer any relief, for since they had been pulled out of their natural orbits by his attraction, they were under a like necessity. Though they were all sure that if they could but study the Catholic faith they would find therein redemption, they had not the time to read or even to find out what books they ought to read and how to get hold of them. Wistfully they debated among themselves how they ought to proceed. It was mentioned, perhaps with deliberate restraint, that Ambrose was too busy to advise them. The only hopeful prospect they could see before them, which indeed offered a very pleasant contrast to their plight, lay in the possibility of inducing one of their more powerful friends to procure them some post, and of then making a sensible marriage with a wealthy wife.

To this Alypius at first demurred. He was a gentle soul to whom one's heart goes out through the ages because of his confession that, though he had sternly refused all bribes when he sat on the Assessor's bench in Rome, he had been sorely tempted to take advantage of the custom by which praetors got their books at cut prices. He had also, much earlier, been the hero of an endearing adventure in Carthage, when he was arrested because, coming on the scene of an interrupted burglary, he had wondered why the burglar was running away so fast and why he had left all those tools lying about, and was thoughtfully examining them when the police came and fell into a natural misapprehension. On him had been bestowed the gift of chastity, for he had, Augustine says, 'made a trial of that act in the beginning of his youth, but having not engaged himself by it, he was sorry for it rather, and despised it.' He saw, therefore, no excuse for introducing the complication of marriage into such a colony of philosophers as they had planned, ten strong, with a rich friend from Thagaste as patron, governed by two officers annually elected, 'whilst the rest were quiet.' But Augustine would not have it so. He urged that many great and good men had pursued wisdom in the married state, and that he himself could not live without sexual intercourse. It was his habit to write of himself as if specially ferocious lust had been his governing characteristic, though a man who was faithful to one woman for fourteen years in a community where temptations abounded and moral judgments were lax cannot really have been the prey of uncontrollable sensuality. But such were his representations that Alypius, always very amenable to argument, admitted that perhaps he had formed his adverse opinion of sexual intercourse too hastily, and that he was prepared to try it again. So all three looked for deliverance to a moneyed marriage.

All this reads like harmless chatter in a garden, the construction of castles in Spain; but suddenly it precipitates into real and very ugly fact. Abruptly Augustine tells us that negotiations were begun for his marriage with a suitable bride, and, thanks to Monnica, were soon concluded. This involved his separation from the woman with whom he had lived for fourteen years. She was packed off home again to Africa. That she was not a loose woman, that their relationship had been serious, she proved by taking a vow of celibacy. It is, of course, possible that the loss of Augustine may have inflicted no great hardship on her. After fourteen years of companionship with a violent and blundering man, the pain of separation might well have been assuaged, and even rendered unnoticeable, by the new-found pleasure of tranquillity, and the peace of the religious life may have seemed to her an exquisite self-indulgence. What is indefensible in the incident, what makes it seem a sickening outbreak of barbaric cruelty amidst all this talk of religion and philosophy and this gluttonous enjoyment of culture, is the separation of the woman and her child. The boy Adeodatus stayed with Augustine and Monnica.

Nothing can make this incident other than horrible; but examination reveals possible causes for it which make it not so wanton and gratuitous as it might appear in its beginnings. It is plain that the moving spirit in the incident was Monnica. Augustine tells us so, and he proves it when he speaks of the departure of his concubine as something that was done not by him but to him. 'When that mistress of mine which was wont to be my bedfellow, the hinderer as it were of my marriage, was plucked away from my side,' he says in a sentence which would arouse our sympathies by its conclusion —'my heart cleaving unto her was broken by this means, and wounded, yea, and blood drawn from it'—were it not that neither then nor at any other time does he utter one word of sympathy with the sufferings of the woman. It can hardly be doubted that he was a passive agent, it is unlikely that he would not have had fortitude to persist in it in despite of these feelings. But while one may accept his story of Monnica's responsibility, one cannot accept his explanation of it. He says that she wanted him to be married so that his sexual life could be regularised and he could be baptized; but that really will not do. If that had been her motive, she would not have chosen him a bride who was so young that there could be no question of marriage for two years, which means that she was probably about twelve or thirteen. For she must have known that with Augustine's strong views on his sexual insatiability he would be bound to take a concubine to fill in the intervening two years, and that the baptism would therefore have to be postponed for that period. A wholehearted interest in his baptism would have led Monnica to search for a bride who was immediately available.

There must be some other explanation, and it is probably of a financial kind. In writings dated a short time after this period, Augustine describes himself and his family as having been in dire need, and one of his letters written in later life speaks explicitly of the smallness of his patrimony, and declares that in entering the Church he passed from poverty to wealth. Out of a meagre estate Monnica was obliged to provide not only for herself and to help Augustine, Adeodatus, and his mother, but to support entirely another son and daughter. For Augustine was not, as the parts of the *Confessions* dealing with his childhood and youth would lead the reader to suppose, an only child. The flat omission of any reference to his sister, and of any but a late casual reference to his brother, gives point to his uneasy description of jealousy in children of tender years. He must have enjoyed cutting these other claimants on Monnica's attention out of the literary perpetuation of his life, cancelling their existence with his pen. Such love would make him long to be dependent on his mother in every possible way, and he would ignore as long as he could her complaints that she found it beyond her power to provide for him. But no doubt the disturbed economic condition of the country caused a failure of supplies that at last convinced him. Moreover, Monnica was probably in a nervously exhausted state which forbade her carrying her accustomed burdens, for the Empress Justina had become an Arian heretic and had harried the orthodox Christians of Milan, until Ambrose, fortunate indeed if he were a seer, and not blameworthy if for once the artist became a charlatan, discovered in a vision the remains of two martyrs beneath his church, and thus proved himself the object of divine favour. Since the cupboard was bare, and since her son would not enter the Church and become a priest, the tired and desperate woman can have seen no hope for the family except in a rich marriage for him; and the dismissal of the concubine would inevitably follow, since the parents of the bride would obviously insist on the rupture of any long-standing tie. The situation has occurred again and again in every society where men marry for money; innumerable plays and novels have shown us the worried dowager forcing her son to send away his beloved mistress and take a rich wife. What is a little startling is to see the drama enacted by persons who were subsequently raised to the status of saintship.

Augustine was in a peculiarly bad state to suggest any alternative to the scheme. Since he had arrived in Milan he had developed enormously in some respects, but in others had regressed. He had become more and more unwilling to cope with his environment, he had become more and more desirous of withdrawing from adult life and settling down in dependence on someone. This was indeed a very profound tendency in him, which went much further than merely wanting to live in a little closed colony on the bounty of a patron. In the *Confessions* he addresses God in very curious terms: 'And thou art my Lord, since thou dost not stand in need of my goods.' Much later he recommends Heaven to a catechumen by the odd promise that not only will he never feel ill or tired or needy there, but no one else will either, so that he will never be under any obligation to do anything for anybody. This fundamental determination to take and not to give explains why he never performed any action during his seventy-six years which could possibly be held up as a pattern for ethical imitation; and at this point it certainly determined his sexual life. A very short time afterwards he writes of the desirability of a wife as consisting entirely on the condition that 'by means of her ample patrimony, it were possible that all those whom you wish to have living with you in one place could be comfortably supported, and that by this reason of her noble birth she could bring within your easy reach the honours necessary for a man to lead a cultured existence'; and in his accounts of his conversations with Alypius he expressly states that though they wanted to be married, they felt no desire to have children or fulfil any of the duties of family life. In other words, what he wanted to do in marriage was not to accept responsibility but to find someone to be respon-

sible for him; not be a father, but to be
dependent on a woman as a child on its mother.
This desire was so strong that he would fall
in with any plan that would punish the woman
who had proved to him that he was not a child
by making him father; and it would give him
great pleasure to take that child from her and
hand it over to his own mother, with whom
they could then live as if they were brothers
instead of father and son. And though Monnica may have initiated the plan for other reasons, her feeling of superiority to other women
shows that she had an intense desire to be the
only woman, which must have been gratified by
its consequences.

Once the deed was accomplished all should
have gone well. Yet Augustine was miserable.
The thing in him that wanted to go back and
be a child was not all of him; there was a thing
in him that wanted to be adult, and this raved.
He took another concubine, but still ached for
the companion of fourteen years. A dark sentence hints that he found he had unleashed
again the homosexual tendencies which had
troubled his boyhood. But, worst of all, what
he had done seemed senseless. Now that ease
and honour were within his reach he began to
doubt their value. Even the need to search

for wisdom seemed not so imperative. 'Nor did I desire as now to be made more certain of thee, but to stand firmer in thee,' he writes of this time. In his depression he went to visit Simplician, a priest of great reputation, who had received Ambrose into the Church; if Augustine could not get attention from Ambrose, he would get it from one who was as a father to Ambrose. He told Simplician in what spiritual difficulties he found himself, and mentioned that he had been reading Victorinus' translations of Plotinus and Porphyry, and at that Simplician rejoiced, for he regarded the Neoplatonists as powerful auxiliaries to the Christian faith, and had himself baptized Victorinus. Proudly he told the story of that distinguished conversion. Victorinus had been the fine flower of pagan scholarship, and such a mighty mocker of Christianity and champion of the gods that his statue had been placed in the forum, an honour usually conferred only on men of action. He had been converted to the new faith by studying the Scriptures in order to prepare a philosophical campaign against it, but at first could not bear to kick away the foundations of his life by a public avowal. Not for long did his fine mind permit him the weakness of suppressing the truth, and he chose to make his profession as publicly as possible. 'So soon therefore as he was mounted up aloft, every one that knew him whispered his name to one another with the voice of congratulation. And who was there that did not know him? And there ran a soft whisper through all the mouths of the rejoicing multitude, Victorinus, Victorinus.' Augustine's record of it shows how he was thrilled by the story of this philosopher who set aside all the highest pagan honours for this subtler form of acclamation, which he had evidently found more intense, with that special and alluring intensity of which Christians, apparently, alone possess the secret.

But Simplician could not help Augustine. No outward help, indeed, could solve his problem, which lay now not in uncertainty as to what he should do, but in a paralysis of the will that prevented him doing what he wanted. He knew now that he wanted neither a wife nor a position, that his happiness must lie in celibate membership of the Church. But he drifted on, unable to break any of the links that bound him to the distasteful pursuit of worldly well-being, performing his work mechanically and resentfully, and spending every moment he could in church. Perhaps it was because he was in an alien country that nothing in his surroundings had the power to say the word which would awaken his will from its unnatural sleep. When at last the awakening came, it was an African, one Pontician, who contrived it. He was a court official who called one day on Augustine to ask him some service, and found him sitting with Alypius. While they were talking he picked up a book which was lying on a games table, and was pleased to find, since he was a devout Christian, that it was no treatise on rhetoric, but St. Paul's Epistles. When Augustine told him he read many such works, he began to talk to them about St. Anthony of Egypt, of whom, oddly enough, neither of them had ever heard, though he was an inspiration to the contemporary monastic movement; but from another sentence it appears also that they were unacquainted with the idea of monasticism, which broke on them as a revelation of delight. But it was not the life of St. Anthony which impressed them so much as a story Pontician told about its effects on two of his friends, young men of noble birth.

He had been, he said, at Treves, when the Emperor had gone to see the chariot races; and he had gone with three other court officials to walk in some gardens by the city wall. He had stayed behind with one of the party, and the

75

other two had wandered off and had come by chance on a little cottage where some Christians lived, where they had rested for a while. As they were sitting there they picked up a little book, which was a Life of St. Anthony. They were so impressed by his retreat into the desert to find God that presently one of them cried out: 'Tell me, I entreat thee, what preferment is that unto which all these labours of ours aspire? What are we at? What is it we serve the State for? Can our hopes at Court rise higher than to be the Emperor's friends? And in this Court what is there not brittle and full of perils? And by how many dangers arrive we at last at one danger greater than all the rest? And how long shall we be getting thus high? Whereas if I be desirous to become the friend of God, lo, I am even now made it.' And both he and his friend, being found later by the other two, refused to return to Court and stayed there in the cottage, living the religious life; and the women to whom they were betrothed, on hearing what their lovers had resolved, dedicated their virginities to God.

This story filled Augustine with shame. In its picture of men preferring the honour of Christian baptism to worldly honours it confirmed the moral of the story of Victorinus

which had moved him so strongly. It pricked
his pride and gave him a feeling of sordid in-
feriority to realise that the kind of people he
most respected despised the secular distinctions
which he had pursued all his life long. He felt
ashamed and squalid and foolish, and as soon
as Pontician had gone a kind of frenzy came on
him and he cried out to Alypius, asking what
sickness it was in them which prevented them
from taking part in this movement to the highest. The Epistles in his hand, he rushed out
into the garden, Alypius following him, for he
was afraid to leave him in such a state. They
sat down as far from the house as possible, and
Augustine fell into a passion of rage against his
own inertia. Of doubt there is not a shadow;
God is so entirely taken for granted that He is
almost ignored. The source of his distress lay
purely in the inability of his will to make the
decision to renounce the world. There was a
debate in him between his sexual impulses and
his desire for continency, which ended in a flood
of tears. He rose and left Alypius, and flung
himself down on the ground under a fig tree,
vehemently asking the Lord why He would not
put an end to this period of helplessness.

He was lying thus, shaken with prayers and
weeping, when he heard a voice from some

neighbour's house, a child's voice; it might
have belonged to a boy or a girl. It was chant-
ing in a sing-song, '*Take* . . . *up* . . . *and*
. . . *read!* . . . *Take* . . . *up* . . . *and* . . .
read!' It chanted it over and over again, and
Augustine began to suspect the sound. He tried
to think if such words were part of any children's game he knew, and he could remember
none. He stood up; and he was sure that the
words were a message from God telling him to
take up the Epistles of St. Paul and take the
first text he should read as a sign. Hastily he
rushed back to the place where he had dropped
the book at Alypius' feet, and snatched it up.
The text his eyes fell on read, 'Not in rioting
and drunkenness, not in chambering and wan-
tonness, not in strife and envying, but put ye
on the Lord Jesus Christ, and make not pro-
vision for the flesh, to fulfil the lusts thereof.'
Light flooded his heart; again his will moved
like a living thing.

Intricate was the workmanship of this omen.
It is well to note that Ambrose had been called
to baptism and the episcopate when he was
attending a basilica, in his capacity as Governor,
to quell a riot that had broken out over the
election of a bishop; and a child's voice had
chanted again and again, 'Bishop Ambrose!

Bishop Ambrose!' It is well to note, too, that the Epistles of St. Paul were the foundations of Ambrose's preachings. One might think that the omen might have been more fortunate, for indeed it would be difficult to open the Epistles of St. Paul and not find some encouragement to adhere to the Church, and it would have been better for the world if Augustine's eyes had fallen on a text that added graciousness to purely negative moral admonition and gaunt invitation to enrol under the right banner. Nevertheless it was the sign for which he had waited, and he was free and happy. He cried out his joy to Alypius, who, always willing to follow his friend's lead, took up this new project of sudden conversion as cheerfully and obediently as he had taken up the idea of marriage. The text he drew was, 'Let him that is weak in faith receive.' So together they went back to the house, and found Monnica, and told her they were at last ready to receive baptism. *Exultat et triumphat.* She was at last happy; for, as Augustine says, she knew a much greater joy than she could have had from grandchildren—and indeed she had one of these—since her son was delivered over to her and her way of thinking, wholly and for ever.

V

AUGUSTINE and his friend did not immediately announce their conversion. They could not be baptized at once, for it was then summer, and at that time baptism was administered chiefly during the night between Holy Saturday and Easter Monday; and they shrank from passing the intervening period in the atmosphere of controversy which any avowal of their intention would create about them. But Augustine's tempestuous spirit could not bear this time of prudent waiting, and cut all ties with this hateful life at once. It called to its aid an illness which, by affecting his chest and throat, made it impossible for him to continue teaching. Meanwhile his affairs had been settled so that he could leave Milan. History rarely tells us who picks up the pieces after the great man has gone by, so we do not know who placated the parents of the affianced bride and who dismissed the new concubine, but it was probably Monnica. At any rate, Augustine records no part of his own in these proceedings. In October the whole household were able to go with his mother and his brother and some pupils, all of African origin, to a friend's simple villa at Cassiciacum, which is now Cassago, on the slopes that rise from the Lago de Varese to the uplands known as the Field of Flowers. There he taught and wrote some treatises, which distress one by the intimations of the suppressed artist in him, both in his descriptions of the fruitful Italian autumn and in his amazing character-sketches of his pupils. But they also exhilarate by the spectacle of genius finding its feet on the ground it prefers. They glow with fulfilled happiness.

In April of the year 387, when he was thirty-three years old, he was baptized by Ambrose at Milan, in the company of his friend Alypius and his son Adeodatus. It was a long ceremony. He had attended the basilica daily throughout March and April to receive instruction in the fundamental truths of the faith, which was often imparted by an exorcist, who had power to expel demons. On Easter Eve he kept vigil, and after midnight knelt before the altar and was touched by Ambrose on the ears and nose in what was known as the mystery of opening. Then they went to the baptistery, where they stripped naked and were anointed by the priests and deacons, who afterwards asked them if they renounced the devil with all his works, and the world with all its luxury and lusts, and bade them spit on Satan. Meanwhile the Bishop exorcised the cistern which was then the font, driving out of it the creature of water, and prayed that the presence of the eternal Trinity might descend upon it. Then the clergy went down into the font with the candidates, and the Bishop stood beside it. He asked each candidate, 'Do you believe in God the Father?' and was answered, 'I believe.' Then the candidate was immersed; that is, he was buried. Then he was asked, 'Do you believe in our Lord Jesus Christ and in His cross?' and answered, 'I believe,' and was immersed again; that is, he was buried with Christ, for he who is buried with Christ rises with Him. Then he was asked, 'Do you believe also in the Holy Spirit?' and he said, 'I believe,' and was immersed again; that is, by manifold lustrations they wiped out their manifold lapses. Then the Bishop sprinkled drops of an unction made of oil and balsam on the heads of the candidates, and announced that thereby God had remitted their sins and called them to life eternal; and afterwards he and the presbyters washed their feet. Ambrose approved of this rite, which was not universal, because he thought that though the sprinkling of the head might remove the sins of the individual, this washing of the feet was necessary to remove his hereditary sins. Then the newly baptized were dressed in clean white robes and given candles to carry. They must have been dazed with excitement and fatigue following on a fast of three days; and a frenzied routine must have streamed past them, for hordes were pressing in to take advantage of the Church's salvation at this time. To complete the rite, the Bishop laid hands on them and called down on them the sevenfold gifts of the Spirit. Then they went out from the baptistery in procession to the basilica, and at the Easter Sunday mass received for the first time the bread and wine of the Eucharist.

But when Easter week was over and Augustine was no longer under the necessity of attending the basilica in his white baptismal robes for mass and vespers each day, he and his mother and brother turned their backs on Milan and set out for their own country. Alypius and a new-found friend, Evodius, went as well, and were with him in the intention of founding a religious house somewhere near his home in Africa. Behind them Italy was crackling like dead wood set alight. The usurper Maximus was gathering his hordes; only a few weeks later he was to cross the Alps and sweep down on Milan, while the Roman Emperor fled first to Aquileia, then across to Thessalonica, on a long journey that ended only in captivity and death. By June, Augustine and his companions had reached Ostia, the port of Rome, and were living together in a house remote from the bustle of the harbour, resting quietly until their ship should set sail. They were all, one feels as one reads Augustine's record, exhausted and happy. One day Augustine and Monnica were sitting by a window that looked over a garden, and as they talked their happiness soared to a climax. They forgot the distressful past, the struggles he had had, and the struggles she had had with his struggles. They talked of the purity of life with God, unstained by sensuous experience, and they were lifted up towards it.

'And when our discourse was once come unto the point, that in respect of the sweetness of that life, not the highest pleasure of the carnal senses, bathed in the brightest beam of material light, was worthy neither of comparison nor even of mention, we, cheering up ourselves with a more burning affection towards that Self-same, did by degrees course over all these corporeals, even the heaven itself whence both sun and moon and stars do shine upon this earth. Yea, we soared higher yet, by inward musing and discoursing upon Thee, and by admiring of Thy works; and last of all, we came to our own souls, which we presently went beyond, so that we advanced as high as that region of never-wasting plenty, whence Thou feedest Israel for ever with the food of truth, and where life is that wisdom by which all these things are made, both which have been, and which are to come. And this wisdom is not made; but it is at this present, as it hath ever been, and so shall it ever be: nay, rather the terms to have been, and to be hereafter, are not at all in it, but to be now, for that it is eternal: for to have been, and to be about to be, is not eternal. And while we were thus panting and discoursing upon this wisdom, we arrived at a little touch of it with the whole effort of our heart, and we sighed, and even there we left behind us the first fruits of our own spirits enchained unto it, and we came back to the sound of our own voices, where words uttered have both a beginning and end. For what is like Thy Word, our Lord, which knows no change, which is without age, and makes all things new?'

The ecstasy does not fall, it rests in the air, circling in its strength. 'We said, therefore: If to any man the tumults of the flesh be silenced, if fancies of the earth and waters and air be silenced also; if the poles of heaven be silent also; if the very soul keep silence within herself and by going beyond the self surmounts the self; if all dreams and imaginary revelations be silenced, every tongue, every sign; if everything subject to mortality be silenced—yea——' Augustine is writing ten years later, but at the recollection of this ecstasy his flesh is swept with a tremor, his words fall into confusion, it is hard to untangle the Latin—'if all these be silenced and He speak alone, not by them but by Himself, so that we may hear His own word; not pronounced by any tongue of flesh, nor by the voice of the angels, nor by the sound of thunder, nor in the riddle of a resemblance, but by Himself alone (and lo! we two now strained ourselves and with rapid thought touched on that Eternal Wisdom which is for ever over all)—could this exaltation of spirit have continued without end, and all the other lesser visions been quite taken away, and that this exaltation should ravish us and swallow us up, and so wrap the beholder in these more inward joys, so that his life might be for ever like to this very moment of understanding which we now sighed after: were not this as much as Enter into thy Master's joy? But

86

when shall that be? Shall it be when we shall
all rise again though nothing of us will not be
changed?'

It was the peak of Augustine's experience. It
is perhaps the most intense experience ever
commemorated by a human being. Some,
however, have doubted if it were distinctively
Christian, and have considered its lack of any
reference to the personages or doctrines of his
new faith as proof that he was still a Neoplato-
nist at heart, and that this was but an ecstasy
such as Plotinus had achieved in full paganism.
But their doubts are groundless, since even the
most devout Christian mystics have found that
only lesser visions and revelations bear traces
of the detail of their faith. The highest state
of mysticism is bare of everything but the
knowledge of God. Yet Augustine himself lets
us doubt whether religion had been the sole
cause of the excitement he and Monnica had
felt. He himself makes us wonder whether
what happened to them at the window was not,
in part at least, an extraordinary manifestation
of ordinary human love: whether the souls of
Augustine and Monnica had not known then
such a peaceful mutual adaptation of the will,
such a severe identity of purpose and process,
such a triumphant duplication of the might of

the self by absorption of another self as all men
seek from birth to death. For he says: 'Such
discourse we then had, though not precisely
after this manner, and in these self-same words,
yet, Lord, thou knowest, that in that day when
we thus talked of these things, that this world
with all its delights grew contemptible to us,
even as we were speaking of it.' This is a curiously apologetic sentence. It suggests that when
he came to write the *Confessions* he had fallen
into the habit of expressing everything in religious terms, but that his violent honesty had
tugged at him as he described this particular
intense experience, and reminded him that
really it was not so; and the particular point
in which he assures us his account is truthful
is a very small part of the whole. Our sus-
picions are confirmed when he continues: 'Then
said my mother: "Son, for mine own part I
have delight in nothing in this life. What I
should do here any longer, and to what end
I am here I know not, now that my hopes in this
world are spent. There was one thing for
which I sometimes desired to be a little while
reprieved in this life; namely, that I might see
thee become a Christian Catholic before I died.
This hath the Lord done for me, and more
also, for that I now see thee having contemned

88

all earthly happiness, to be made His servant;
what then do I here any longer?" ' This reads
very much as if it were the first time religion
had come into the conversation by the window,
as if they had been speaking till then only of
their life on earth. But to suspect a human
basis for the experience is not to belittle it or
to deny that its ultimate significance for Augustine was religious.

Perhaps it was because the marsh-fever was
already on Monnica that she felt the weariness
of life; perhaps it was that which had fanned
her being to the flame that had ignited them
both. Five days later she was gravely ill. She
was a bad subject for such a malady, or rather,
it was in a position to do her a great service.
She was fifty-five, and her middle years had
been spent in a tedious struggle for money and
an effort to get her brilliant and helpless son
on his feet. On the ninth day she lost consciousness; and when she came to herself she
looked up at Augustine and his brother and
said, 'Here you must bury your mother.'
Augustine was silent, but his brother bade her
take heart, since she had better not lay her
bones in a strange land, and think of going
home. She looked sadly at him, and then
turned to Augustine, saying, 'Hark at him!'

Then she exhorted them to bury her anywhere, but always to remember her at the altar of the Lord. After that the progress of her malady silenced her; but she had said enough to put Augustine into a blaze of joy. Always before, Monnica had been at pains to make sure that she should be buried beside her husband. She had had a grave made ready beside his, so that she might enjoy his company in death as in life, and that her neighbours might hand down the tale of how God had granted her to travel far beyond the seas and to lie at last under the same earth as her man. Augustine thanked God that out of the fullness of His goodness He had thrust this empty conceit out of his mother's heart. She was not changing her plans because of the fatigue and delirium of her sickness. When she had talked about dying, at the window before she had begun to ail, she had said nothing about being buried in her own country; and later he heard that she had told some of his friends in his absence how little it mattered to her where her bones rested, since no place was far from God. It was in full sanity that she was giving him her body to bury alone, in a country where she had never been with her husband, where she had travelled only for her son's sake. Fervently he thanked God for having worked this miracle, which removed an ancient offence, which at last made all things seemly.

But he had to pay a price for this violent and final delight. His mother lay dead, and he had to close her eyes. As he stood with the tears of agony running down his face, the boy Adeodatus broke out into loud cries. His mother had been sent away from him the year before, and now the only other woman in his life had gone; he himself was to die a year later. They turned and silenced him. Had they not the promise of Monnica's immortality? They were feeling sad only because 'the most sweet and dear custom of living with her' had been too suddenly broken. Augustine tried to comfort himself by remembering that in her last hours she had called him a dutiful child, and had boasted that he had never uttered a harsh word to her. But a dead body presents its case against the world with tremendous forensic power. He saw that whatever honour he had paid her was as nothing compared with her slavery to him. Though Evodius took up the Psalter and began to sing, and the Christian brethren came to put all things in order for the burial, he could not loosen the constriction of this pain at such thought. But his pride made him tearless, then and at the graveside, though his agony would not be abated even when he reminded himself that Christianity had wiped out death and substituted for it immortality. He went out from the burial-place to have a bath, telling himself with pathetic pedantry that the Greek word for bath meant that which drives sadness out of the mind. But he learned that sorrow cannot be sweated out. In bed, however, he slept, and woke a little comforted, with some lines from a hymn written by Ambrose ringing through his head. The words came out of the darkness like a kind, fatherly message, and he began to know the relief of prolonged weeping.

It is odd that the two stories he tells of his mother when he writes of her death, to prove what a miracle of holiness then passed, both end in violence. The first refers to Monnica's early married life. Her mother-in-law, it seems, was prejudiced against her by the tale-bearing of some servants, but she had kept her head so well and behaved with such patient good temper that in the end the mother-in-law had reported the servants to her son, who had them well beaten. The second is a grim and ugly anecdote of Monnica's childhood. There had been in her father's house a privileged

servant, one of those horrid old women that by
length of service and toadying to the elder mem-
bers of the family win the right to bully and
torment the others.   It was her malicious pleasure to forbid the children to drink water between meals, at which they got a severely
rationed supply.   Her reason for this restric-
tion, which was sheer cruelty in thirsty Africa,
was that if the children got into the habit of
drinking water freely when they were young,
they might drink as much wine when they were
older.   So when little Monnica was sent down
to the cellar to draw wine for her parents, she
used to take a sip for herself; and this habit
grew on her till she found herself taking whole
cupfuls.   She was not detected by her parents
nor by the old woman; and the habit might
have grown into a disposition towards drunkenness, had not one day a maid with whom she
used to go down to the cellar lost her temper
with her and hit her savagely on the teeth, calling her a little sot.   This unpleasing sequence
of events seems to Augustine a beautiful proof
of the Lord's wisdom that can 'by the fury of
one soul thus cure the ill custom of another.'

These stories make a strange tribute for a
loving son to lay on the grave of his mother;
but perhaps that tribute records a perception

that even as Monnica was calm, so too is the heart of the whirlwind. She was modest and sober and restrained as a Christian woman should be; but she survived like a conqueror, and all about her that was not of her way of thinking fell like the conquered. Patricius had long been in the grave. In Augustine's mind she had annihilated great men and vast cities: Virgil and Mani had passed like blown wraiths, the walls of Carthage had fallen, it was as if Rome had never been built. Even the world of flesh about him she seemed able to alter and destroy. Milan was no longer the pompous seat of the Imperial Court; it was an inn at which he had stayed on his roundabout journey home to her, and it had closed its doors after he had gone. All the land through which he had passed was wiped out now as if it had served its purpose and was needed no more. All Italy, all paganism, all profane existence was going up in flames. Monnica alone was left victorious, and her death did not put an end to her victory. It only meant that as she swept the board of this world, so she was to sweep the board of infinity and eternity. Years later, when Augustine was considering the transmigration of souls, he writes: 'Plato has declared, to be sure, that human souls return to earth after death to the bodies of animals. Plotinus also, Porphyry's teacher, was of like opinion, but Porphyry rejected it; and that very rightly. He believed with Plato that souls pass into new bodies, but into human bodies. Doubtless he shrank from the other opinion because he saw that if it were true, a woman changed into a mule might carry her son astride her. He forgets that his own system means that a mother changed into a young girl might make her son incestuous.' Others, thinking of transmigration, might see a myriad of souls in flux about the generative gates to earth, but not so Augustine. For him these souls did not exist. For him there was then and thereafter to be nothing in the universe save his mother and her son.

VI

THE time of Augustine's genius had come. There was nothing but his mother and her son in the universe, but she was not in the visible universe. Therefore she must be in the invisible universe. This laid him under the urgent necessity to prove beyond all shadow of doubt that the invisible universe existed, to study the plan of its structure and the nature of its substance. He had received the stimulus which was to make him one of the first four Doctors of the Church. But he could not settle to his work at once. For he missed the summer sailings of that year, went to Rome, where he wrote several treatises against the Manichæans, and did not complete his journey to Africa till the following August. This delay must have gone against the grain, and he nowhere explains how he came to submit to it; but some have suggested that he was recalled for the purpose of writing these treatises by Siricius, the new Pope, who was a great harrier of the Manichæans. Once in Africa, Augustine went to Thagaste and wound up his father's estate, and used his share as a foundation for a small religious house, the first Augustinian monastery. There he lived very happily for three years, writing busily, confirming himself in the possession of the Christian tradition, and preparing himself to hand it on and extend it by his own work; and there he might have spent all his days had it not been for the tendency of his age to call on its men of thought to be men of action.

It happened that in the seaport town of Hippo Regius, which is now Bône in Algeria, a high official told someone that he thought he might have strength to renounce the world if he could but talk with the monk Augustine; and this came to Augustine's ears. He set out to help this convert with an easy mind, for Hippo was among the towns he could visit in safety. Involuntary episcopacy is one of the few perils which man has been able to eradicate since the time of Augustine, and it is hard for us to realise that it was then a hovering terror, almost as the press-gang once was in England. Not only was the Government official of high character liable to be called on to perform duties and take vows towards which he felt no inclination, but also the religious man who had found his proper vocation in the monastic life was apt to be forcibly transferred to the way of service he had already rejected. Augustine, therefore, took pains to avoid, in any travels he had to undertake, all towns which were without a bishop. But he went to Hippo in perfect confidence, and even lingered there when his convert showed signs of vacillation, because it possessed a worthy bishop, one Valerius, and no town was allowed two bishops. It was unfortunate that Valerius was a Greek, who was far from fluent in Latin and knew no Punic at all, and was therefore of little use to a population that spoke Latin and Punic; and that advancing age was depriving him of the power to show any compensating ecclesiastical merits. The congregation badly needed an energetic and learned pastor who could preach against the heretics and schismatics that were seriously threatening the existence of the Catholic Church locally, and who could bring money to the treasury to enable alms to be distributed. Augustine's fame had spread over the countryside very quickly. When he came to the basilica they knew they saw the man they needed, and they determined to get him by ordaining him as a presbyter, though that did not quite give them what they wanted, since in the Western Church presbyters did not preach. They seized him and dragged him by force to the altar, crying, 'Augustine the presbyter! Augustine the presbyter!' After that there was no help for him, though Augustine wept aloud. It shows what an air of pride the man must have had, that those around him assumed he was weeping because he had been made a presbyter instead of a bishop. But his tears came from a deeper cause. Thereafter his work of establishing the existence of the invisible world was to be interrupted by appeals that he should establish the continuity of the visible world; and he was to run backwards and forwards between the two tasks, making adjustments in the visible world according to his conception of the invisible world, and altering his conception of the invisible world according to his experience of the visible world. This cannot be regarded as a misfortune. The capability he showed in his new duties proved that he had an immense amount of energy to spend in action, and if this had been given no outlet the atmosphere of the religious house at Thagaste might well have become so tense that it would have remained the last as well as the first Augustinian monastery. The abduction of Augustine by the congregation of Hippo was probably most healthful for his genius.

These new duties were more onerous than Augustine can have feared even when he wept, for Valerius set aside Church custom and made him use his mastery of the Latin tongue in the pulpit. He had to preach constantly, at least once a day, and his dramatic temperament obliged him to make each sermon an important performance. One of his most vivid letters describes with what thunderbolts he preached down the custom of merrymaking in the grave-yards and churches on saints' days; thus he introduced into Africa the prohibition which Ambrose had forced on Milan, which Monnica had cheerfully obeyed. In the same letter one learns of animated correspondence with the Primate of Africa. He was becoming an expert player of the administrative game. Besides these duties he had to give much time to the instruction of catechumens, a task which he came to perform with the joy of the virtuoso, as one may see in his treatise *On Catechising the Uninstructed,* which is still the best handbook ever written for people who have to speak over and over again on the same subject and so run the risk of boring themselves and other people. Soon he had to bear the whole burden of the see on his shoulders, supervising the Church property, organising charitable relief, and acting as *Cadi* to disputants, for Valerius was afraid that his able presbyter might be stolen from him by some bishopless town, and he persuaded the Primate of Africa to override precedent and allow Hippo to have two bishops. The Primate of Numidia for a time opposed the consecration of Augustine on the grounds that he had used magic to secure to himself the possession of a female penitent, but this accusation seems not to have cast the shadow over the proceedings that it would have done at a later date. After the story had been disproved, the Primate showed eagerness to make amends by himself consecrating Augustine.

The grip of the visible world on Augustine was strong, but he, being one of the strongest among the sons of man, could throw it off. He had founded in Hippo the second Augustinian monastery, and there he lived. Every moment that he could, he went to his cell and shut out all thought of his priestly duties, and the scene where he fulfilled them. This last exclusion must have been a great effort, for the scene was very beautiful. Hippo was a little Naples, set in a blue bay, and behind it was a plain, rich with vineyards and olive groves and farm-lands, and watered by a river that wound down through piney heaths from an amphitheatre of

wooded mountains on the south. From innumerable vivid phrases in Augustine's writings, which escape him before the censor at the
back of his brain can act, we know how that
landscape and the life it nourished delighted
his strong senses. But he cancelled them with
his will, and on the nothingness which was left
in their place he drew another landscape, another life, which were not an atom less real
because they could not be seen. Why, the seen
world depended for its reality on the unseen.
He points out that parents and children could
not believe in each other's love if it were impossible to believe in the unseen, and then
society would fall apart, and man pass away.
Nor need the unseen remain the uncompre-
hended. He smote his own breast, and knew
he knew who smote and who was smitten; he
anticipated Descartes' *Cogito, ergo sum,* and
matched the self of which man is certain against
the most extreme uncertainties man recognises
in the universe, as if he were cheering two
cocks fighting in a pit. It was a spirit very necessary in that period when—as happens in all
periods of extreme political and economic disorder—the proper philosophical scepticism as
to the infallibility of man's mental instrument
had suffered a morbid degeneration into hys-

terical coma. He stoutly maintained that consciousness could investigate its own laws, and that that was worth doing, which the Sceptics had come very near to denying. He glorified reason, and bade us put 'far from us the thought that God detests that whereby He has made us superior to other animals, far from us an assent of pure faith which should dispense us from accepting or demanding proof.' But he insists that faith should precede reason. At first this seems contradictory and lacking in faith, which surely should hold that since the truths of religion really are truths, reason is bound to lead to them. But, in fact, this proposition reveals Augustine's astonishing power as an introspective psychologist. He perceived that reason, the working of the conscious mind, was not a mechanical process which inevitably turned out truth as its finished product. There was something else in a human being which decided what reason should work on, and how it should work, and unless this something decided that the finished product should be truth it might well turn out to be a mere rationalisation of error. He was able to realise this because, as his attempts to define memory show, he was well aware of the existence of an unconscious mind; and that realisation must have been given point by his knowledge that, if he had tried and failed to find truth during his twenties, it was because this hidden part of his nature had preferred to remain in error. Hence he had cause for maintaining that unless the whole of a man gave allegiance to a theory of values which recognises knowledge of the truth as an essential good, he could not be trusted to use his reason with integrity; and as for him Christianity was the means by which such a theory could be propounded to the whole of man, his argument that faith should precede reason has a sound psychological basis which it is not easy to dispute.

It was difficult to draw the map of the invisible world on the blackness of nothingness; and he bore heavily on the outlines that one whom he had loved and trusted had traced before him. There can be recognised in the Augustinian system the distinctive draughtsmanship of Ambrose. The sermons of Ambrose dealt much with sin, which, since he was greatly influenced by Greek thought, he regarded as not-being, and rejected with a Stoic passion for the good life. The root of sin was regarded by him not as sensuous, not as a mere matter of fleshly appetites, but as situated more deeply, in man's perverse use of his free will. Only could its root be torn up if man won through his faith in Christ the right to lay hold on the strength of God. Again and again he cries out humbly and proudly that the soul must not boast because it is upright, but because it has been lifted up by the Lord; and if these passages are translated—left untranslated their distinctively Italian Latin is a guide—it is hard to believe that they were written by Ambrose and not by Augustine. For that position was the foundation of Augustine's system, though he added to it the quality which one would expect from the drama which had led him to the creation of that system, the quality which Ambrose could not have contributed, and probably would not if he could. He added to it his characteristic ardour. He suffused the existing Christian system with a greater passion of love than it had known since the immediate influence of its founder had passed away. In the intervening centuries the sense of God as a judge who tried man on moral grounds had degenerated into a too narrowly legalist attitude towards religion; it was felt that salvation was a matter of the performance of a contract between God and man, whereby retribution was demanded and merit was supplied. But now Augustine depicted the relationship between

God and man as being passionate and eventful
and subject to woeful alienation followed by
happy reconciliation, like the relationships of
the flesh.

But though the saints have decided that sin
has not its roots in the flesh, it can hardly be
denied that thought springs from that soil.
Augustine was never more bitter than when he
was denouncing those who represented God as
having human form and human passions, yet all
his conceptions of God are determined by the
passions which are imposed on humanity by its
form. We know, not by deduction but from
Augustine's own statement, that his most intense experiences were those arising out of the
relationship between himself and his parents.
It is not surprising that he depicted the relationship between man and God, which must
inevitably engender the intensest of all experiences, as a magnified form of the relationship
between a child and its parents. Always it had
been understood that by the operation of God's
grace Christ had the power to abrogate man's
sins; but Augustine made it appear that God
continuously rained grace on mankind, continuously transforming him from the filthy subject
of original sin to one bearing resemblance to
God, even as parents love their children and

train them up from angry helpless babes to civilised adults. Man attains resemblance to God, but is never the same as God, just as a child grows up to be an adult like its parents, but never becomes its parents. While it grows it shall bask in love, but that love can be withheld if the child is not good, and even if it is. With a curious wild gesture, that passed on to the invisible world the guilt of not declaring its ultimate motives which lies so heavily on the visible world, Augustine laid down that God's love can be withheld for reasons beyond man's comprehension.

He invented the doctrine of predestination: which is the doctrine that God chooses some to be saved, and some to be damned. This is, of course, not a question of judgment by faith or by works. For since man can hold forth or achieve works only by God's grace, it follows that he can lack them only by God's determination to withhold His grace. There must be justice in this, but the cause is not communicated to the victim, it remains God's secret. 'When of two infants, whose cases seem in all respects alike, one is by the mercy of God chosen to Himself, and the other is by His justice abandoned: why, of these two, the one should have been chosen rather than the other, is to us an insoluble problem.' He found his sanction for this idea in the preaching of St. Paul, but to explain his warm liking for it one need only look to the nursery and see if a beloved child does not sometimes feel an intensification of its rapture at thinking of other children not so loved, and that for no other reason than that they are they. Yet, since a child must believe its parents morally right, it must believe their action in withholding their love to have some moral justification. It must believe them right in all things, if it is fully to participate in the most grievous and joyous of all experiences, the cycle which Augustine has made the pattern of Christian piety. The child must be naughty and run away, get dirty and hungry and tired, and know the terror of loneliness and a pricking conscience; and then suddenly be picked up and carried safe home again, to be washed and fed and rocked to rest, to be loved and forgiven. So the mystic sees himself as the child of God, playing truant in time and the finite, being brought home to the eternal and the infinite.

But how can this condition of things have come about, if God is omnipotent? For then He must have permitted, nay, even caused, the preliminary aberration, the sins that occasioned the repentance. This was a terrible charge. For though Augustine had the lightest possible sense of ethical responsibility, he had the heaviest possible sense of sin. Regarding the consequences of his actions he was as indifferent as almost any man who has been self-conscious enough to record his own emotions, but he had an excessive share of that feeling of guilt which exists quite unrelated to any individual experience in the mind of almost every human being. It seemed to him as if humanity was saturated with the obscene, not by reason of what it did but of what it was; and his years in the Manichæan camp had confirmed him in this attitude. He could not bear to think that God could be the author of this filth by which he was haunted, and he set himself to shift the responsibility on to man's will and the fall of Adam. To do this he had to create a complete philosophical system that must explain every phenomenon of the invisible and visible worlds. Though that system is not entirely satisfactory, though it abounds in false assumptions and contradictions, it still remains one of the most stupendous works of man. Augustine's errors were the result of his position in time, and so are not disgraceful. It was for him to be the great romantic artist, leaning far out to the apprehension of yet unformulated truths, and bringing in the false mingled with the true in an immense mass of material which was reduced to order eight hundred years later by the great classical artist, St. Thomas Aquinas. We have here one of the first and most impressive demonstrations that all classicism depends on a previous romanticism.

But from this task Augustine was perpetually called away to the routine of his episcopal office. As the state of disorder in Africa grew wilder his sermons had to be more and more authoritative and dynamic, more and more catechumens pressed forward for instruction, the administration of the Church funds became more complicated: when a man left his money to the Church instead of his kin, Augustine was constrained to return it for fear that heretics and schismatics should gossip, but had to face the anger of those in his flock who needed bread. There was Church discipline to be maintained. He had, for example, to deal with two deacons who had accused each other of attempted seduction. He sent them together on what must have been a very embarrassing journey to the tomb of St. Felix of Nola in Italy, hoping that the relics of the saint would make some discriminating gesture. There were also fussy parishioners who had rather more conscience than ought to be in private hands. 'May a Christian use wood taken from one of the idols' groves which have been chopped down as part of the State campaign?' asked one Publicola. 'May a Christian put a wall round his property for defence against an enemy? And if some others use that wall as a place to fight and kill, is he then guilty of homicide?' 'If a Christian buy in the market-place meat which has not been offered to idols, but rather suspects it may have been, and in the end decides that it has not, does he sin if he eats it?' Augustine answers, 'Better not! Yes! No! No!' and wearily gives reasons, but obviously refrains only with difficulty from adding, 'and try not to be so silly.'

The correspondence for which he had a greater taste was of the kind which he initiated with St. Jerome six years after he had gone to Hippo; though that took a turn which he hardly enjoyed. Jerome was a saint in the highly technical sense of the word, being a literary genius of repellent disposition and venomous tongue. But he was like the juggler who was found performing his tricks before the Virgin's altar because he had nothing but his professional skill to offer up to her. Such as his qualities were, he laid them without reservation at the service of his religion. He was fifteen years older than Augustine, and was a famous scholar who still kept the world busily admiring him and hating him even though he had retired to a monastery at Bethlehem when the correspondence between them started. A rumour had spread abroad that Jerome was translating the Scriptures from the original Hebrew into Latin, and this came to Augustine's ears. He wrote to Jerome, begging him to abandon this enterprise and to confine his attention to the Greek Septuagint translation of the Scriptures, and calling him to account for having ascribed a pious fraud to St. Paul in his interpretation of a perplexing passage in Galatians. His letter arouses tenderness and apprehension in the reader. It is as if one watched a St. Bernard puppy, as yet unaware that cats do not like dogs, gambolling up to make friends with a Persian. But it is also an abominable letter. Augustine was no scholar at all compared with Jerome; he was the newly appointed presbyter of a fourth-rate diocese, while Jerome was a world-renowned religious leader; they were strangers. Yet Augustine's approach to him would be considered pert and familiar even in a close friend and equal. He expresses doubt whether the Greek translators can have left so many points unsettled that Jerome thinks it worth while translating them all over again. 'Now, these things were either obscure or plain. If they were obscure, it is believed that you are as likely to be mistaken about them as the other translators. If they were plain, it is not likely that the others should have been mistaken about them. Having stated the ground of my perplexity, I appeal to your kindness to give me an answer regarding this matter.' He went on writing letters in this strain for years, careless of the fact that Jerome did not answer them. 'Wherefore I beg you,' he says, 'apply to the correction and emendation of your book a frank and truly Christian severity, and chant what the Greeks call a palinode. For incomparably more lovely than the Grecian Helen is Christian truth. I do not say this in order that you may recover the faculty of spiritual sight—far be it from me to say you have lost it!—but that, having eyes both quick and clear in discernment, you may turn them towards that from which, in unaccountable dissimulation——' and so on.

There is more here than simply a failure in manners. There is a failure to be civilised. Augustine shows no signs of realising that Jerome, like himself, was working under the direction of conscience, that he had his own approach to truth which might even afford as good results as Augustine's, and that he might be hurt by an attack on his life-work. Worst of all, he exhibits towards Jerome that kind of sadistic indelicacy which lays impudent fingers on hidden wounds. It happened that, some time before, Jerome had parted from his life-long friend Rufinus after one of those bitter quarrels that spring up between specialists. Jerome believed that Rufinus had betrayed that obligation of honesty which binds scholars, and, what was more, had involved him in this betrayal, so he turned and rent him. This was, as Jerome's writings show, a source of agony to him; the quality of his venom always suggests that his cruelty was a defence put up by an extreme sensitiveness and need for love. It seemed to Augustine good that he should intervene in this private matter. 'If I could anywhere meet you both,' he exclaims unctuously, 'I would throw myself at your feet, and there, weeping till I could weep no more, I would appeal with all the eloquence of love——' and so on. These indiscretions were punished by Jerome in a series of masterpieces of murderous irony which make Wilde and Whistler seem clodhoppers and Voltaire and Gibbon mealy-mouths. He had even greater justification than the content of the letters, for Augustine had allowed copies of them to be widely circulated through the Church before he had waited to make sure that Jerome had received them and had an opportunity to answer them. It was therefore very handsome of Jerome to write a year later holding out his hand in a good-natured gesture of reconciliation. But Augustine used a clumsy and ungracious misinterpretation of a charming phrase of Jerome's—'Let us play in the fields of scripture without wounding each other'—as an excuse for a priggish rejection of his advances.

Looking back, one sees that Ambrose may have had his reasons for not reciprocating Augustine's affection; and in a letter to Jerome Augustine tells a vivid story which reveals what weariness and irritation must have afflicted the more urbane type of churchman at this time. In Oea, which is now Tripoli, a certain bishop was reading the Scriptures to the congregation, using Jerome's version, and came on the passage in the book of Jonah in which it is described how the Lord God caused a plant to grow into a lofty shelter for the disaffected prophet. The plant named in the original text is a kind peculiar to Asia, and the earlier translators, in a desire to make the passage intelligible to Europeans and Africans, had called it either a gourd or ivy; and while the Septuagint translators had chosen the gourd, Jerome chose the ivy. The congregation had been previously accustomed to use the Septuagint version, and when the point came in that admirable short story where they had always heard the word 'gourd' and they heard 'ivy' instead, they were angered, like children who are listening to a familiar fairy-story and are told that instead of three bears three gazelles came into the little house in the wood. But these were dangerous children. They raised a riot in the basilica, and the terrified bishop had to let them send out for the opinion of the Jewish residents in the town as to the meaning of the original Hebrew word; but this opinion was given less in care for philological accuracy than in the hope of prolonging Christian dissensions, and in this it was entirely successful. It must have been infuriating for a learned man like Jerome to have it suggested that he should gag his scholarship lest it should offend such foolish assemblies of the childish and the unlettered; and the incident reveals how unjust it is to regard Christianity as a mob-religion that wiped out the individualised culture of paganism. The cleavage between the mob which wanted to reduce everything to the level of their own rudimentary understandings, and the individuals who wanted those who could extend human knowledge to be given full licence to do so, was as marked within the Church as without it. The State had bred a vast part of its population simply to do the dirty work of the world, and now that it had lost the power to regiment this artificially created army of inferiors they wandered loose and looting over the whole social system. One of the most interesting of Augustine's writings, from a historical point of view, is his treatise, *Concerning the Labour of Monks,* which deals with the problems created by the monks who refused to obey the apostolic injunction that they should support themselves by their own hands, and who claimed the right to live like the lilies of the field and rely on alms from the faithful. These monks, it appears, were either workmen who could no longer face the impossible struggle for subsistence, or the freed slaves of landowners who had been obliged to free them on becoming Christians, and who may have become Christians for the express purpose of being able to hand their properties over to the Church and disembarrass themselves of the intolerable burden of taxation. The Church, which was yet inexperienced in handling the problems arising out of monasticism, gave itself no liberty to turn away these workmen and freed slaves if they declared their desire to be monks; but it was perfectly aware that when they refused to work they were actuated by other than religious considerations.

Africa, indeed, was groaning like a rotten branch that high winds are tearing from a dying tree. Gildo, a Moorish prince of savage genius and immense wealth, who had been made military governor of Africa in reward for his apparent fidelity to Rome, had covered the land with the horrors of revolt from 394 to 398; and from the Imperial edicts which for ten years after deal with the rebels and informers against them one may learn of the horrors involved in the suppression of that revolt. The subdued provinces had suffered the worst punishment that can be inflicted on rebels. They had no confidence that their conquerors would continue to rule them. For the Goths were coming down on Italy slowly and irresistibly as age, and the Vandals were following them as death follows age. But all this was as nothing to Augustine. Though he was young in the Church, and though Hippo was a diocese of little importance, he had become the mind of the African

Church, and when heretics and schismatics put forth false doctrine it was from him that a lead was expected. He had to deal again with Manichæanism, and he shows again a curious lack of sympathy for all its doctrines save its belief in the evil of the flesh. He attacks Mani's poem about the universe as if it were a literal statement of fact, and it is as if a clever counsel were bullying Dante. 'But can you point us out on the map these places you say you visited, Heaven, Purgatory, and Hell? Are you aware that the measurements you give of this place are not mathematically credible?' But the treatises are interesting to a modern reader, because they will very often make him feel as if he were watching a Tolstoy who developed much further than he actually did, rebuking a Tolstoy at the stage at which he stopped. When Augustine points out that there is really much more to the religious life than giving oneself gooseflesh over the fact that some things strike one as dirty and others do not, it appears as a grave indictment against the nineteenth century that it allowed itself to be impressed by a teacher whose experience was limited to only a small part of Augustine's spiritual progress.

The Pelagian controversy came later and occupied him longer. Pelagius, a monk, and

Celestius, a pious layman, came forward with propositions that struck at the bases of the Augustinian conception of religion, which were again and again to be revived and to contend with it throughout the next fifteen hundred years. They held that man's will is free, and that he can use it to become virtuous and be rewarded by God. This is a superficially attractive proposition, and its prophets laid it down because the moral stagnation of Rome made them feel that virtue must be preached anew. But it has the disadvantage of lacking, even from the least orthodox point of view, full correspondence with reality. If we examine ourselves carefully we cannot claim to have free will. We exercise what looks like a free faculty of choice, but the way we exercise that faculty depends on our innate qualities and our environment, and these always bind us in some way or another to the neuroses which compel us to choose death rather than life. We cannot break this compulsion by the independent efforts of our minds, for they cannot function effectively unless they learn to depend on tradition. Augustine's view that we are full of original sin, that we do not enjoy the free use of our wills, and must link ourselves to the eternal if we are to be saved, is at least a symbolic interpretation of something that the most secular-minded must allow to be true. Since the triumph of Pelagianism would have meant not only the establishment of an inexact psychological statement but the limitation of Christianity to a narrow Puritanism, it is as well that Augustine was at hand to fight it. His lack of ethical interests made him, perhaps, not such a deadly opponent as he might have been if he could have fought Pelagius and Celestius nearer their own ground. But the intellectual problems involved were delightful to him, though sometimes they baffled him.

For instance, what was the origin of the soul? It was necessary to know for certain. For if the soul of each infant is generated by the souls of its parents as its body is generated by their bodies, then it inherits its spiritual as well as its physical attributes from Adam, and it is natural enough that it should inherit the sinfulness brought about in him by the Fall. But if the soul of each infant is newly created by God, then where does its sinfulness come from, since God could not possibly create evil? Augustine was obliged to confess that he did not know. But he told two bishops who asked him that perhaps Jerome knew, and that they had better write to him and find out. It says much for the older man that he and Augustine were again on friendly terms. Later on, Augustine himself wrote Jerome a long letter asking him to confirm his belief in 'that most firm and well-grounded article in the faith of the Church of Christ,' that new-born children can be delivered from perdition only by baptism. But Jerome sent no very satisfactory answer. He replied courteously to the bishops. With the exquisite capacity of compression which comes of long and disciplined use of the pen he set down the various theories regarding the origin of the soul, but could go no further. He manages just one flick of the pitchfork and flourish of the forked tail to show that the old imp in him is not dead yet. The bishops, he says, had better apply to 'that holy man and learned Bishop Augustine, who will be able to expound you his opinion, or rather, I should say, my own opinion stated in his words.' More than that he could not do. There had been a time of late when he had been so miserable that he had forgotten his own name, and had kept silent, knowing it a time for tears. He had been forced to lay his studies on one side till his eyes were less constantly dimmed with weeping. For he was an old man, over seventy, and he could not bear such ill news as the Sack of Rome by the Goths.

No man had cursed Rome more roundly than
Jerome, but no man had been more aware of
it. The hard brightness of its street-scenes,
and the tumult of its human babble and its
traffic noises, assault the senses from his page.
Such intense consciousness is usually the effect
of love: and though it is sometimes the effect
of hate, such hate is not very far from love.
Whether he loved or hated the place, it had
been his home for many years, and now it was
gone. To tell him how completely it had gone,
men and women whom he had known as rich
and powerful passed hungry and footsore by
the gates of his monastery at Bethlehem, content to beg if they might find safety in the
sacred places of the Holy Land. But he did
not believe safety was to be found any more
upon earth. It had died at the heart. After
Rome had fallen, had not the Arab tribes
seethed in rebellion across the desert so that
he and his brothers and sisters in God had
trembled for their lives? He knew much more
than an old man's terror at these mishaps. For
he too had believed in the creation of an invisible world, though almost certainly he had
not believed that it could be achieved all at
once by one excited man. He had seen it being created touch by touch, not by successive

generations of men, who would correct each other savagely if need be and error crept in, but who would persevere in the great task with perfect loyalty, age in age out. But they could not do that if they were fighting for their lives with Goths and Arabs. And if they could not, what would be the good of their lives? They would die like beasts, not knowing their own nature or purpose. So he did not answer Augustine's letter to him about the origin of the soul, nor yet his later one on the saying in the Epistle of St. James, that 'whosoever shall keep the whole law and yet offend in one point, he is guilty of all.' For the years did not take from him his horror at the Sack of Rome.

But the news affected Augustine very differently. He was not appalled by it. In his sermons he made a shrewd guess that it was not such an immediate catastrophe as might be supposed, and that the congregation he addressed need fear no immediate alteration in their state; and this was indeed the case. But had Africa lain under an immediate menace he would have been reluctant to admit it, for the news had filled him with a passionate exaltation. He was as happy when he heard of the Sack of Rome as he was when his mother no longer wanted to be buried by the side of his father.

To commemorate his emotion he turned aside
and wrote, ostensibly to answer the charge that
Rome had fallen because the gods were angered
at the apostasy of their people towards Christianity, a book called *The City of God,* and
though he took many years—probably thirteen
—to write it, there is the same intense glee in-
scribed on the last page as on the first. That
glee is not to be dismissed as malignant, though
that it certainly is in part. It is also one sign
of the vigour of a conflict which engendered
enough dynamic power to make *The City of
God* a work of genius. For that it certainly is,
though it is also a shocking and barbarous book.
A student is reported as having said of it that
'this is not a book, it is journalism; whenever
St. Augustine had nothing else to do, he sat
down and wrote a bit of it'; and if he erred in
too roseate a conception of the journalist's life,
he conveyed correctly enough the sense of extreme incoherence which baffles and even dis-
gusts the ordinary reader of this book. The disgust arises, perhaps, because there is here more
than the formlessness which was imposed on
Augustine by overwork and liability to inter-
ruption. There is also the disorder which
comes from abandonment to a base passion.
Though Augustine was a saint and a genius and

a most lovable child of earth, he was often not a gentleman, and he is never less gentlemanly than in his jeers at the plight of the Romans and his ill-natured allegations that all their virtues were really vices. Elsewhere in one of his letters Augustine lets fly an accusation at the pagan world which touches the spot of its rottenness. 'These learned men,' he called the philosophers, 'whose ideal of a republic or a commonwealth in this world was rather investigated or described by them in private discussions, than established and realised by them in public measures.' But in *The City of God* little enough of the criticism of the pagan world is on such high ground. There is a wholesale rejection of all the treasures of art and science, of law and organisation, that Greece and Rome had laid up for humanity; it is like seeing a giant child wrecking a museum. There are innumerable cheap jokes against polytheism, flushed and interested researches into obscene rites, and ungracious attacks on the Platonists.

Yet tangled up with these is wisdom, and more than wisdom. There is a sudden magnificent attack on Imperialism. He sees and presents in perfectly ordered paragraphs—though these are scattered far apart in irrelevancies—the psychological advantages that small States

enjoy compared with great Empires. The conquering spirit that had made Rome cross the
seas to Africa is destroyed in a blaze of fiery
criticism. It was loutish stupidity. It had not
the dignity of evil pride, it was more mockable
than that, it had defeated its own ends, and had
led straight to ruin and this sweet Sack of Rome.
Such States as do these things, being without
justice, are loathly things, mere robber bands;
and in a State without God there can be no justice, for justice and all such things come of
God. Yet the State cannot be wholly of God,
because it is caught in the coarse foul mesh of
material reality. Yet it must be. For without
States there could be no kings and emperors,
and kings and emperors can do what no common man can do to punish the heretics and
schismatics that lay villainous hands on the faith
of the Church of Christ. He flags, he ram-
bles, he reverts to his unfortunate wistful ob-
session about the means of generation that
would have been possible had man's constitu-
tion been ever so little different. But his genius
restores him. He sees again a vision such as
he and his mother saw when they leaned from
the window, a little time before she died, having
accomplished all that she could do for him.
It was a vision that showed history as the mass

movement of predestination, as the organisation in grace of those whom God has chosen not for their merits but out of His goodness, to enjoy not war but peace, not sin but beatitude.

'Accordingly, two cities have been formed by two loves: the earthly by the love of self, even to the contempt of God; the heavenly by the love of God, even to the contempt of self. The first glories in itself, the second in the Lord. The first seeks glory from men, but the greatest glory of the second is God, the witness of conscience. The one lifts up its head in its own glory; the other says to its God, "Thou art my glory and the lifter up of mine head." In the one, the princes and the nations it subdues are ruled by the love of ruling; in the other the princes and the subjects serve one another in love, the latter obeying, while the former take thought for all. The one delights in its own strength in the persons of its rulers; the other says to its God, I will love Thee, O Lord, my strength. Therefore the wise men of the first city follow either the goods of the body or mind or both, and those who have known God glorified Him not as God, neither were they thankful but became vain in their imagination, and their foolish heart was darkened, professing themselves to be wise.

But in the other city there is no human wisdom, but only godliness, which offers due worship to the true God and looks for its rewards in the society of saints, of holy angels, as well as holy men, that God may be all in all.'

VII

It might seem that the victory was wholly with Monnica and the Church. Yet it was not so. In the forty-four years of life that followed Augustine's conversion he never for one minute ceased to be the loyal servant of Christianity and the active enemy of paganism; but the nature of man is so constituted that it can contrive the extremest treacheries without itself knowing what it has done. We must suspect a profound and subtle form of such treachery when we notice the change that passed over Augustine's character after middle life. He retained the curious quality which made him lovable in spite of his complete egotism. That one can see from his friends' letters. But in other respects he knew a complete reversal of his previous tendencies. When he tells the fussy enquirer, Publicola, that 'as to killing others in order to defend one's own life, I do not approve of this, unless one happen to be a soldier or public functionary, acting not for oneself, but in defence of others or of the city in which one resides, if one act according to a lawfully given commission and in a manner becoming that office,' we may smile at the brisk official tone, and may mark what seven years of the priesthood have done to the scholar who in youth was sealed and dumb with individualism. We must laugh aloud when, fourteen years later, he writes in a letter discussing the evils of demon-worship: 'Apuleius, though born in a place of some note, and a man of superior education and great eloquence, never succeeded, with all his magical arts, in reaching, I do not say the supreme power, but even any subordinate office as a magistrate in the Empire.' It is true that this sentence has some justification, considering Apuleius' worldly ambitions, but the old Augustine would surely have reflected that the demons had given Apuleius his genius, that might be reckoned as supreme power. The mind of the new Augustine seems to have taken an official turn; and letter after letter, treatise after treatise, shows that it had. He had become a conservative. He stood by the organisation, he felt under an obligation to make it work. The importance of making it work outweighed the importance of making his own psychical organisation work. So he became hurried, impatient, high-handed. He became, in fact, Patricius.

Year by year he gradually transferred his allegiance to the ideals of his father, which had been associated with the State, adherence to Rome, and the cultivation of a robust antithesis to the Christian ideal of meekness and passivity, while he apparently continued to serve the ideals of his mother, which had centred round the Catholic Church; and how he did it can best be illustrated by his relations to the Donatists. These were schismatics who already had a long history behind them. When Diocletian was persecuting the Christians in 305, the magistrates were obliged to demand that the Christian clergy should surrender their sacred scriptures for destruction. The clergy that refused were slain. But Mensurius the Bishop of Carthage thought of a neat evasion, and he and his archdeacon Cecilian presented the magistrate with a selection of heretical writings. Thus they gained safety for themselves and their congregations; but several years afterwards, when Mensurius died and Cecilian was made bishop in his place, a number of Numidian bishops objected on the ground that the two had really handed over the sacred scriptures, and that Cecilian was therefore a 'traditor'; and that this made it impossible that he should be consecrated a bishop, since only sacraments administered by a righteous priest were valid. This contention, after being debated in many courts, was quashed. It had the sole merit that it might have done something towards raising the character of the priesthood; otherwise there was little to be said for it. The evidence in the particular case debated was weak; and the underlying principle was illogical, since the real dispenser of the sacraments must be Christ, and it is inconceivable that a relationship decreed by Him can break down through the personality of the mediator. Moreover, it destroyed the continuity of the Church as an imaginative conception, to be replaced by a wild and uncomforting fantasy. One might as well say that people would lose their capacity to appreciate art if the artists of one generation failed to attain a certain standard of proficiency. But worst of all were the practical effects of the schism. Christian communicants obviously could not suffer themselves to be deprived of the means of grace, and if they were liable to suspect that this was happening on account of the behaviour of their priests, the Church would have become a bear-garden.

It indicates the misery of Africa that such a poor and unattractive schism should have gained a whole army of adherents. Its original power

is said to have lain in the circumstance that
though Mensurius and Cecilian had not handed
over the sacred scriptures, a great many other
ecclesiastics had, and were eager to avert suspicion by accusing other people of their fault.
But its later strength was drawn from the poverty of the land. There were a vast number of
Africans who were submerged in suffering by
their economic conditions, and who consequently needed a religion that glorified suffering. This they had found in the Catholic
Church when it was a persecuted religion; but
they found it there no longer now that the
Catholic Church was the triumphant ally of
the Roman Empire. Many such people joined
the Donatists for no other reason than to find
themselves again in a harassed minority, and Augustine's writings suggest that the Church
itself had been partly to blame for this by
its emphasis on the cult of the martyrs. These
schismatics were joined by a number of desperate people, who formed bands called *Circumcelliones*. Scholarship handsomely offers us the
choice of translating this word as either 'the
chaste ones' or 'those who hang round the huts.'
They were, in any case, hungry African na-
tionalists who hated the Roman power which
had let them be born into this ruin, and con-

sidered themselves justified in robbing and murdering the oppressing classes. The Donatists had no relish for these allies, and tried to cast them off. In 340 the Numidian Donatist bishops had appealed to the Roman military governor to send troops against the local Circumcelliones, and after the pitched battle outside Octava that followed they would not permit the bodies of the rebels to be buried in the basilicas. But the forces drawing them together were strong. Two commissioners, Paul and Macarius, were sent from Rome to bring the schismatics back to the parent church, and they made themselves as well loved in Africa as Cromwell in Ireland. A silence fell; but it was the sign of sullen fear, not death. The country was still hungry and governed by aliens. Then Julian the Apostate came, and ordered the restitution of the churches to the Donatists. They came back like a pack of wolves for their revenge. But after three years he was gone, and the Catholics were taking revenge for that revenge. Imperial edict upon Imperial edict beat down the Donatists, while the misery of the country brought them more and more recruits. When Augustine came back from his sojourn in Italy there were Donatists in almost every African town, and in many places, including Hippo, they outnumbered the Catholics.

There could be no satisfactory method of dealing with Donatism. It raised problems of which no solution has ever been found; for there can be little doubt that the prime causes of the movement were economic. There is room for debating how far and how drastically it was necessary to deal with it. The opinion that sacraments were valid only if administered by righteous priests was unsound, but so little offensive that St. Cyprian had held it till the day he died; and in all other respects the Donatists were rigidly orthodox. They were, therefore, disseminating no very dangerous poison in the public mind, and one would have thought that Augustine and his friends could easily have preached down their single and obvious error. But once a Church acquires property, and takes over administrative duties from the State to the extent to which Christianity had done during the fourth century, schism becomes not only a difference of opinion about ecclesiastical organisation but an attempt at malversation. It is as little a matter for tolerance as an attempt of certain shareholders in a company to take out their capital and seize part of the company's plant. Nor could tolerance have been stretched far enough to excuse all the doings of the Donatists. One cannot believe all the accusations brought against them by their opponents. Augustine's tales of their immorality are the same sort of thing he told about the Manichæans, and the evidence of his contemporaries goes to show that in this he was unjust. In reading patristic literature one's incredulity is constantly aroused by the frequency with which persons holding unsound doctrines are also guilty of the grossest misdemeanours, often of kinds that one would think most incompatible with strong religious interests. Other accusations against the Donatists are frivolous. Augustine's famous story of the Donatist baker at Hippo, who would not bake bread for Catholics, proves on examination to have taken place forty years before he wrote, during the terrorist period under Julian the Apostate. The Donatists' desire to avoid social intercourse with their enemies was such as the world has since seen mutually displayed by Jews and Gentiles, Catholics and Protestants, Anglicans and Non-conformists; so it cannot be taken as proof of exceptional naughtiness. But there can be no denying that many of them thieved, burned churches, beat people with clubs, threw vitriol over bishops, and murdered their opponents; and the standard of civil order was so low that they could do these things with impunity.

Augustine's treatment of Donatism was therefore determined, and not very pleasantly determined, by two essential facts: that the Church could not exercise tolerance towards it, and had to perform the duty of suppressing its offences against order. What is significant is the spirit in which he carried out this treatment. It was in no way different from the spirit in which his father, or any other good Roman citizen, would have waged war against rebels who had risen against the Empire. The extent to which Augustine had changed since his youth can be measured by the contempt he pours on Donatism because it was purely African. In the early days of his return to Thagaste he had formidably rebuked a pagan scholar of Madaura who had reproached the Christian Church with provinciality and had jeered at the Punic names of some of the martyrs. Later he himself jeered at the Donatists, because their church, which had for headquarters in Rome only an insalubrious cave presided over by an obscure bishop, had neither the majesty nor the magnitude of his own church, which was coincident with the Empire. He begged the question at issue as

Imperialists do when they deal with rebels: he treated it as a crime in his opponents that they resisted his authority, and ignored the arguments by which they tried to prove that authority lay not in him but in themselves. He was growing to find the arguments of others as negligible as people do when they can back up their own by force, for he had the ear of the Court, which was now at Ravenna, and could inspire the promulgation and enforcement of edicts providing for the imprisonment, expropriation, physical chastisement, and exile of all heretics and schismatics. Like a bluff old soldier, inured to the rough justice of campaigns, he recommends the application of this medicine to the lawless and the law-abiding alike. 'As to those who had not, indeed, a boldness leading to acts of violence, but were pressed down by a kind of inveterate sluggishness of mind, and would say to us, "What you affirm is true, nothing can be said against it, but it is hard for us to cast away what the tradition of our fathers has handed down to us," why should not such persons be shaken up in a beneficial way by a law bringing upon them inconvenience in worldly things, in order that they might rise from their lethargic sleep and awake to the salvation which is to be found in the unity of the

Church?' He was indifferent to the effects of
the persecutions he was thus initiating, not because he was cruel, but because his imagination
had completely disappeared, as it sometimes
does in men of action. The extremists among
the schismatics were passing through an epi-
demic of suicidal mania which bears heart-
rending witness to their misery. They did not
care how they died so long as they died. They
insulted judges so that they should inflict the
death penalty, and waylaid travellers whom
they forced to kill them, threatening them with
death if they did not. Those who died thus
at the hands of others hoped for a martyr's
crown; but others were amply content merely
with death, and drowned themselves, threw
themselves over cliffs, or set themselves alight.
To these unhappy creatures Augustine addressed priggish rebukes, or was mildly facetious
at their expense. To a Donatist priest, who,
to avoid arrest and forced conformity, first threw
himself down a well, and then, when he was
arrested and put on a horse to be taken before
the authorities, flung himself down on the
ground and inflicted grave injuries on himself,
Augustine wrote a brisk and cheerful letter,
beginning, 'If you could see the sorrow of my
heart and my concern for your salvation, you

would perhaps take pity on your own soul. . . .'

With the Conference of Carthage in 411, which was the reward of Augustine's efforts, and brought together the beaten Donatist bishops to go through a travesty of reconciliation with the Church, he rejoiced as one cannot imagine a trained philosopher rejoicing at an intellectual assent extorted by force. Nor did he show doubt later, when his firm way with schismatics brought blackness into a situation dark enough already. Heraclian, the Governor of Africa, who had rebuffed a part Gothic, part Roman, rebel expedition which had sailed from Italy in 410, himself became a rebel, and in 413 took a fleet to the Tiber. He was routed, and was beheaded at Carthage; and again unhappy Africa was subjected to the miseries that attend the suppression of a revolt. Count Marinus was sent to discover and pass judgment on all Heraclian's supporters, and his commission gave endless opportunities to the informer who wanted to satisfy a judge. So the Donatists denounced two brothers who were both State officials and had been active in the enforcement of the Imperial decrees against schismatics. One had been President of the Conference at Carthage. Though they were innocent of any share in the revolt, they were suddenly exe-

cuted. There is a letter from Augustine to
the official whom he believed to be responsible
which is an outburst of rage like a thunder-
storm: like one of those outbursts for which
his father was famous in Thagaste. But he
shows no sign of recognising that perhaps a
Capitoline type of tragedy follows from a Capitoline policy of oppression. It might be said
that in that lack of recognition he was of his
time, and therefore no blame attaches to him.
But that is not true. He had come from Italy
with other views, which permitted his first letters on the Donatists to be kindly and tolerant;
and they were still held by others. 'Reflect,'
Nectarius writes to him, 'reflect on the appearance presented by a town from which men
doomed to torture are dragged forth; think of
the lamentations of mothers and wives, of sons
and fathers; think of the shame felt by those
who may return, set at liberty, indeed, but having undergone the torture; think what sorrow
and groaning the sight of their wounds and
scars must renew. And when you have pon-
dered all these things, first think of God, and
then think of your good name among men.'

There was nothing but violence in his life
in the visible world, even when he turned from
baiting heretics and schismatics. The church

at Hippo was very different from the quiet church to which Monnica and Ambrose had led him. What it was may be judged from the curious letters that passed after Melania and Pinian had visited him. Melania was the heiress of one of the wealthiest families in Rome, and when the Vandals had drawn near she and her husband Pinian and her mother Albina had started on travels which eventually led them to their African estate, which was near Thagaste. They were enormously rich. It is said that they owned estates not only in Rome, Africa, and in several parts of Italy, but also in Sicily, France, Spain, and Great Britain. They were also very pious, and made such gifts to the Church that they ultimately beggared themselves. They became very friendly with the Bishop of Thagaste, who was Augustine's old friend, Alypius; and when Augustine wrote to them excusing himself from visiting them on the grounds of his bad health, the severity of the winter, and the fretful exigency of his congregation, they persuaded Alypius to take them to Hippo. But when a visit to the basilica was proposed, Pinian, as a precaution against the peril of involuntary priesthood, made Augustine promise not to ordain him even if the congregation demanded it. It is relevant to note that Augustine, though himself a victim of compulsory ordination, had come in a very few years to apply it himself; there exists a very sinister letter in which he bids one Castorius try to like being a bishop, since that is certainly what he is going to be.

Pinian's precaution was, however, of no avail. The congregation immediately recognised the wealthy and pious visitors, and shouted to Augustine that he must forcibly ordain Pinian as presbyter; and when Augustine told them of his promise they were damped only for a minute, and suggested that he should either break it, or evade it by arranging for another bishop to perform the ordination. Meanwhile Melania and Pinian fled in terror into a recess in the choir. Augustine flatly refused to do the mob's bidding, saying that if they insisted he himself would cease to be the bishop, and then a riot broke out. It was so severe that, as Augustine admits, he was alarmed for the safety of the buildings, and dared not take Alypius through the crowd, because they were shouting insults at him for having forestalled them and secured the rich man for his own congregation, and seemed likely to attack him. While Augustine stood facing this disorder and wondering what to do, Pinian sent a monk to tell him that he wanted to swear to the people that if he were ordained he would at once leave Africa. But Augustine saw that this would only make the crowd more dangerous, and while he was pondering what to do he received another message from Pinian, who, alarmed by the increasing tumult, offered to withdraw this defiant oath and make the more conciliatory promise that he would consent to settle down in Hippo, provided he were not forcibly ordained. Augustine went to discuss this offer with Alypius, but he, doubtless remembering the occasion in his youth when he was found minding the burglar's tools, and reflecting that he would have to face not only Pinian and his wife but his notoriously forceful mother-in-law Albina, tersely replied, 'Please don't ask me.'

Augustine then saw nothing for it but to announce this second promise to the crowd, who, however, accepted it only with the shrewd proviso that Pinian must also promise that if he were ordained it should be in their church. Augustine went back and put this to Pinian, and they set about framing the terms of the oath. Pinian insisted on certain conditions being stated to cover such necessities as might compel him to leave Hippo, and of these he named first of all an invasion of barbarians. It must be remembered that these unhappy people had fled Rome before the Goths, and that rebellious Africa was known to be half-hearted in her own defence. But Augustine objected to this condition, on the curious ground that the people would regard it as a prophecy of evil; and Melania was not allowed to mention the possible effects on their healths of the climate, though a Roman lady might well have shrunk from permanent residence in North Africa. Finally Pinian insisted on including a general clause to cover all necessities, but Augustine was right when he warned him that the mob would not tolerate it. When the clause was read, such a riot broke out that the terrified Pinian eagerly took an oath without reservation to become a permanent resident of Hippo and be ordained there or nowhere. At this 'the people recovered their cheerfulness once more,' and after giving thanks to God, demanded that the oath should be properly signed and witnessed. Pinian gave his signature, and when Alypius and Augustine were urged to witness it, 'not by the voices of the crowd, but by faithful men of good report as their representatives,' Augustine was willing to do so. But Melania sternly forbade him to put his episcopal signature to such a discreditable document. From her gesture we can see how profoundly shocked the Roman visitors were by those African disorders; and it is characteristic of Augustine that he records the rebuke without realising its significance. Once the oath was recorded, the people let the party leave the church, and by the next day all three visitors had fled back to Thagaste. Once there, Pinian and Melania did not hesitate to declare that there could be no question of keeping an oath extorted in such circumstances, and to make the most definite allegations that not only had the congregation of Hippo shown unpardonable cupidity in attempting to kidnap a wealthy stranger, but that Augustine had acted as their accomplice.

Of the full force of this accusation Augustine must be acquitted. He had not wanted the Romans to come to Hippo; his invitation to them had been so lukewarm that it might have been taken as a hint that they should stay away. But he was guilty of a great deal. Even Alypius, lifelong slave as he had been to his admiration for Augustine, felt that this time his idol had gone too far, and when he got home he sat down and wrote a stinging complaint against the threats and insults to which he had been subjected at Hippo, and the blackmailing of Pinian. How much justice was on his side can be judged from Augustine's bland and unscru-

pulous replies to Alypius' and Albina's re·
monstrances. He makes no apology for the
shocking manners and morals of his flock, nor
for his own failure to have them under control,
and mentions with an air of satisfaction that
only one of the monks from his own monastery
took part in the riot. He minimises their offences. 'Even if there were mixed in the crowd
some who are paupers or beggars, and even if
they did help to increase the clamour, and were
actuated by the hope of some relief to their
wants out of your honourable affluence, even
this is not, in my opinion, base covetousness.'
And as for the oath: 'Tell me, I beseech you,
what hardship deserving the name of exile, or
transportation, or banishment, is involved in
his promise to live in Hippo?' So might a
general defend his beloved legionaries. They
may sometimes raise Cain round the camp-fire
and try their hand at a bit of looting and bon-
neting civilians, but that only shows their high
spirits. With an altogether pagan verbalism
he insists that Pinian must keep his oath, since
an oath is an oath however it was extorted. To
give his view a Christian appearance he makes
perfunctory allusions to the Scriptures, but he
speaks much more of the etiquette of the battlefield, of Regulus and his oath to the Cartha-

ginians, and of the Roman censors who refused to inscribe on the roll the names of the senators who had committed perjury even though they were compelled to it by the fear of death. Had not this bluff and jolly buccaneer been a priest, one would never have guessed from those letters that he had even been baptized.

Augustine wrote as one who can think only in terms of Roman order; but as the proceedings at Hippo show, he lacked its substance. His congregation had the licence but not the discipline of soldiery. What dangers were latent in the situation can be guessed from the letter which he wrote to Count Boniface in 417. This is a very long and full recital of the benefits derived from that 'function of Christian charity' known as persecution, which is 'unwilling to spare the brief fires of the furnace for the few, lest all should be abandoned to the everlasting fires of hell'; and interesting as it is in its revelation of how imagination can be killed in a man by cruel duties, it derives still greater interest from the person to whom it is written and the reasons for which he had invited such a letter. Boniface was a Greek who had defended Marseilles against Ataulf and as a reward had been appointed to Africa first as a commissioner to the Imperial Government, then as the military governor. He was an able man, and was both a sincere believer and the husband of a very pious wife. At that time Imperial servants had much reason to profess Christianity, for both the Emperor Honorius and his dominating sister Placidia were devout. Boniface would therefore be moved by temperament, affection, and ambition to accept the orthodox Catholic policy. But it is evident that Augustine's letter was an attempt to allay doubts which were vexing Boniface as an official. It was not quite as certain as might have been wished that the persecution of the Donatists was producing unity rather than disunity: that Augustine's use of the Roman formula was not, considering the special African circumstances, an ultimate injury to Rome. There was to be nothing so simple, in this most complicated man, as a final victory for Patricius.

VIII

ROME needed no further enemies. She had enough. In 416 Wallia the Goth sent a fleet to attack Africa. It was shattered by storms near Gibraltar, and though he had to make peace thereafter to get food for his starving army, and become an ally of Rome in her war with Spain against the Vandals, this was no true victory for the Empire. It registered no recovery of health. About the edges of tortured Africa tribesmen eroded civilisation by their incessant raids. During the next few years the Empire failed at the heart as well. The weak Honorius suddenly turned in hatred against his sister Placidia, and Old Rome stood by him, while all the new barbarian allies on whom the dying Empire had come to depend stood by her. There followed after this a quarrel between Boniface and a general called Castinus. It has been conjectured that the reason for this was that Boniface had been put forward as commander-in-chief by Placidia, and that Castinus was the candidate preferred by Honorius. In any case, Boniface was an unhappy and disillusioned man. His beloved wife had died in 418, and he had been so stricken by grief that he would have resigned his military career and become a monk, had not this intention so shocked and alarmed Augustine that he travelled all the way from Hippo to Boniface's camp in southern Numidia in order to dissuade him. We see the official trend of Augustine's mind in his own description of this interview; it appeared to him Boniface's plain duty to abandon his desire to go into seclusion and cultivate the spirit when he had the opportunity of maintaining the peace and unity of Roman Africa in the Imperial service. But now Boniface found difficulty in going on with his work, since he lost his bid for the command of the forces, though he had made an attempt to consolidate his position among the allies by marrying a barbarian princess, who had to be hastily converted from Arianism to Catholicism before the ceremony could take place. He had to retire to Africa, whence he watched with some satisfaction the defeat of Castinus in Spain, and set up as a pro-Placidian governor. He sent all his revenues not to Honorius but to Placidia, who was an exile at Constantinople, and waited his time.

In 423 Honorius died, but his time did not

come. To keep Placidia and her children out
of power, Castinus, who had still command of
the forces, put on the vacant throne a State official named John; and then he revived his
feud with Boniface. All available forces were
sent against him to Africa. But Placidia's son,
Valentinian, dethroned John and replaced
Castinus by a general called Felix. But still the
time had not come for Boniface. There was
some silly court intrigue, and Boniface was
shabbily rewarded for his loyalty to Placidia,
and, still worse, knew that Felix had conceived
a grudge against him. There can be no exag-
gerating the plight of Boniface, who had waited
so long for order to be restored in Italy, and
then found that it was no order; who had hoped
to be a firm administrator supported by a strong
central government, and who found himself in
a noose at the end of an immensely long coil of
rope. When Felix recalled him to Italy in 427
he refused to go, and stood forward frankly as
a rebel. Gildo and Heraclian had already
shown how inevitable it was for any able-spirited
man to feel that Africa must cut the now unnatural tie with decaying Rome.

The first expeditionary force sent over by
Felix, Boniface defeated easily. But the second, which was composed largely of Gothic

mercenaries, and led by a German general, was more formidable. It was for fear of it, some historians tell us, that Boniface treacherously appealed to the Vandals and let them into Africa: but such historians wrote a century later. The evidence of the one contemporary historian who writes in any detail makes it seem more probable that the Vandals, who had for long been casting covetous glances at Africa and had since 419 moved their headquarters to the south of Spain, had planned an invasion quite independently, and that the contending parties in the State had both tried as a last resort to enlist the support of the invaders. By 425 the Vandals had made a landing near Tangier. Though this was then treated as a part of Spain, and not of Africa, it was near enough to fill any governor with the most piteous and desperate forebodings of a breaking world.

To Boniface, at the time of this rupture with Felix, Augustine wrote a letter which is amazing in its vigour for a man of seventy-six. It is, however, not at all a wise letter, and it illustrates painfully two of Augustine's chief failings in its ill-timed garrulity about sexual matters, and in its inability to realise that other people also had tragedies and consciences. Augustine begins by expressing regret that Boniface should

have married a second time, and claims, in the
blandly unscrupulous tone noticeable in the
letters about Melania and Pinian, that he had
no moral right to remarry, because he had expressed the intention of not doing so in the
interview in the south Numidian camp. 'When
I learned of your second marriage,' Augustine
writes, in the manner of the worst kind of
headmistress, 'I was, I must confess it, struck
dumb with amazement'; yet no oath or promise
had been given. There follows gossip about
concubines, and an allegation, which no com-
mander of forces would find helpful, that many
persons were following Boniface because they
were 'desirous of obtaining through this certain advantages which they covet, not with a
godly desire, but from worldly motives.' It goes
on to complain that Boniface was not dealing
as he should with the invasion of Africa by
savage tribesmen from the interior—('I need say
nothing more on this subject because your own
reflection must suggest more than I can put
into words')—and accounts for this by a thinly
veiled accusation of treachery. These denun-
ciations were for long regarded as weighty evidence against Boniface, but they cannot be
taken seriously by a generation which can remember the speeches made during the war in

which the lesser sort of public man used to account for the Cabinet's failure to do anything
about winning the war by the hypothesis that
it had been bribed by German gold. We know
little of Boniface beyond his early piety and his
grief for his dead wife, but we can guess how
he or any other able man would have felt as
he sat trapped between the Imperial Government, the Vandals, and the tribesmen, and what
a vexation this letter must have been to him;
particularly as he had already begged Augustine
with some impatience not to write of matters
about which he knew nothing.

But there are certain points in that letter
which are significant. One is its discourtesy.
It is amazing that a bishop could with impunity write a letter to the representative of
government in Africa covering him with insults and even making slighting references to
his wife. This was partly due to Augustine's
charm. It is not at all irrelevant to his theological system, with its emphasis on salvation
by grace and predestination, that he was one
of those people who never deserve forgiveness
but always receive it. Monnica he had often
offended, but she counted nothing against him.
We read of him raising the just anger of
Jerome, Alypius, Melania, and Pinian, and then

we read later that they are friends again, though
there was no reconciling tie of blood. But it
was partly due to the position of the Church,
which alone spoke with authority in that world
of collapsing institutions. That Augustine took
advantage of this position to show indifference
to his correspondents' feelings is not altogether
the fault of his egotistical temperament. He
was following a fashion. The early Christians
cultivated aggressiveness as a noble defiance of
the pagan State, an advertisement that they enjoyed heartening knowledge of the next world
and need fear nothing in this. When Cyprian
wrote the letter quoted at the beginning of this
book, there was great courage in his insolence,
for he was addressing the representative of the
power which a few years later cut off his head.
But the tide turned, and the Church became
the ally and even the dictator of the State, far
too quickly for Christians to drop the habit of
insolence when the occasion for its passed.
Hence the curious rudeness that broke out between Christian correspondents when they happened to differ. 'Thou biddest me take back
this lie; cease thou to be a liar thyself,' writes
Jerome to Rufinus, and the passage has many
parallels in patristic literature. Hence, too,
the harshness of language which the orthodox

used of heretics and schismatics, and hence, since it is difficult to use harsh language about a man and retain the capacity to treat him justly, the violence of even those persecutions which were initiated with the intention of suppressing violence. What damage this provocative habit had caused can be guessed from one of the accusations which Augustine made against Boniface. He had, it seems, let some of his household lapse from Catholicism into Arianism, and his infant child had been baptized into that heresy. Since he must have longed for national unity more than anything else, it looks very much as if he had come to doubt whether Catholicism was an unmixed blessing for Africa, and was inclining towards treating the heresies with tolerance. Augustine's lack of such doubts, his comfortable persistence in the habit of rebuke, and his assumption that the situation could be satisfactorily dealt with by determined offence and puritan manners, make him seem by comparison insanely rash, but there must be remembered the strain which that time laid upon the imaginative man. There was innate in Augustine the desire that the world should go up in flames which marks the romantic artist; and this had been stimulated by the apprehension of the age, which Cyprian describes, that the world itself was on the eve of death. This apprehension had itself been inflamed to fever by the chiliastic fantasies of Christianity, its sumptuous visions of the last things and their replacement by the divine.

If Augustine had had full prescience he might, indeed, have awaited the future with composure, since, though the old order was ended, it was to be succeeded by a new one which was, century in, century out, to be dominated by his spirit. It was not only that all the important subsequent manifestations of the religious spirit were to show signs of his influence, that his insistence on the unity of the Church was to confirm Catholicism as his doctrine of predestination was to beget Calvinism. It was also that humanity, and in particular the artist, was to think and feel as much as he thought and felt; that a great many people have recognised a peculiar fitness in the designation 'the first modern man,' which was bestowed on him by two German writers. Augustine took as his subject-matter, with a far greater simplicity and definiteness and vigour than any earlier Christian writer, a certain complex of ideas which are at the root of every primitive religion: the idea that matter, and especially matter related to sex, is evil; that man has acquired guilt through his enmeshment in matter; that he must atone for this guilt to an angry God; and that this atonement must take the form of suffering, and the renunciation of easy pleasure. Instead of attempting to expose these ideas as unreasonable, or to replace them by others, as nearly all the ancient philosophers had done, Augustine accepted them and intellectualised them with all the force of his genius. It would be easy to prove how closely the modern world has followed in his steps by examining the works of its great artists; the Augustinian content of Shakespeare alone is impressive. But the point can be more briefly proven if it be considered that the unique position of Goethe is due very largely to his freedom from Augustinian conceptions; and that to-day, fifteen hundred years after Augustine's death, after a raking attack on the supernatural and a constant search for a rational philosophy lasting several centuries, the greatest artists still restrict themselves to his subject-matter. Lawrence tried to investigate the complex of ideas and test its validity by exposing himself to its emotional effects, which had long been disregarded in the one-sided discussion of its intellectual bases. Proust made a colossal effort to justify his sense of dualism by marshalling all the evidence for the horrid oddity of matter collected by his senses, and to soothe the sting by propounding that experience could be converted into beauty by being removed into the immaterial and therefore clean world of memory. James Joyce in *Ulysses,* representing the spirit by the unstained boy Stephen Dedalus and matter by the squatting buffoon Leopold Bloom, finds a myth that perfectly expresses the totality of facts and emotional effects of the Augustinian complex. It is the ring-fence in which the modern mind is prisoner.

But the content of the artist's mind is not peculiar to itself. Its sole peculiarity lies in its exceptional consciousness of a content which we know it shares with the rest of men, since if it did not, works of art would not be generally comprehensible communications. Since that content is common to all, men of action as well as artists must be dominated by this same deep fantasy of dualism and the need to wipe out guilt by suffering; and perhaps it is this which causes the pain of history, the wars, the persecutions, the economic systems which put many to the torture of poverty and raise up rich men only to throw them down, the civilisations that search for death as soon as opportunities for fuller life open before them. There is confirmation for this suspicion in the life of Augustine, who as an artist and philosopher was so explicitly dualist and tragic, who as a man of action had some hand in a policy that dealt the final blow to a system which had once promised ease to man, and submerged his land in disaster.

In 429 Gaiseric and the whole of the Vandal forces left Spain behind them and launched an attack on Africa. The Romans and Boniface dropped their feud. They tried to make a treaty with the Vandals, but they were no longer in a position to exact consideration. Boniface then went out against the invaders at the head of a force of Romans and Visigothic mercenaries, but he was beaten. The Vandals broke over the country like a wave. There was ground for terror, but the old man did not feel it. We have four important letters belonging to these last months. One is an exultant account of the conversion of a physician named Dioscorus, who had promised to be baptized in panic at his daughter's sickness, but after her recovery had forgotten his vow until the Lord smote him with blindness. During the baptismal rite he omitted for some reason to repeat the Creed, so although the Lord gave him back his sight He afflicted him with partial paralysis and total loss of speech. After he had confessed his omission and written out the Creed, the Lord removed the paralysis, but left him dumb. 'So,' writes Augustine, 'that frivolous loquacity which, as you know, blemished his natural kindliness, and made him, when he mocked Christians, exceedingly profane, was altogether destroyed in him. What shall I say, but "Let us sing a hymn unto the Lord, and highly exalt Him for ever! Amen." ' The second is a letter to an Imperial Commissioner, bidding him remember what he himself seemed sometimes to have forgotten, that 'it is a higher glory to slay war with a word, than to slay men with a sword'; and the third is a touching expression of gratitude, pitiful in its suggestion of old age, for praise that this Commissioner had bestowed on his books. The fourth is a letter to a priest who had enquired of him whether he might forsake his church and flee before the invaders, since he could not see what good he did by waiting to see men slain, women outraged, churches burned, and himself put to the torture. The old man reminds him of the unhappy mob that took refuge in the churches when the enemy were near, crying out in fear, begging for the Sacraments. 'If the ministers of God be not at their posts at such a time . . . !' He himself stood firm at Hippo, though Boniface was soon to retreat to it, though it was soon to be besieged. One remembers the story that the Roman legionaries had told long before, of lions met in the Numidian sands that knew the human tongue. This one could still wake echoes with a good round-mouthed roar, though it was in its seventy-sixth year.

Perhaps there was some truth in the other story that the Roman soldiers used to tell of Africa, the story of pythons that put legions to flight. For as the Vandals swept across the country, out ran the Donatists to meet them, eager to change masters, frantic to avenge themselves on the State and Church which Augustine had made them hate. No defending force could stand its ground against such ubiquitous treachery. The legions had to break and run, vanquished years before by the correspondence which had passed backwards and forwards between Ravenna and Hippo, weaving of complaint and edict and enforcement a shroud for Roman Africa. Augustine had seemed in later life a copy of Patricius, but he used the high-handed, choleric method of Patricius to destroy the system with which Patricius had been identified in his mind. It was as if a python had wound itself round the Roman standard and very slowly crushed it with its coils.

Throughout the siege, the text was on Augustine's lips, 'Righteous art Thou, O Lord! and upright are Thy judgments.' Sitting at table among his monks and the fugitive priests who had come for shelter to his monastery, he uttered the stoic and not specifically Christian prayer: 'I ask God to deliver this city from its enemies, or if that may not be, that He give us strength to bear His will, or at least that He take me from this world and receive me in His bosom.' Presently it became apparent that the last part of his prayer was to be answered, and he took to his bed. He would have driven the world out of his cell, but a man brought him his sick son to cure by the laying on of hands. Augustine answered bluffly that if he had any power to cure the sick the first person he would use it on would be himself. The man persisted, however, that an angelic voice had told him to make the demand. So Augustine laid hands on the boy, and he was cured; but the old man was not yet to be allowed his rest, for there came to him petitioners who wanted his prayers for some who were possessed by devils. At that Augustine burst into tears. He prayed very vehemently for the afflicted, and the devils went out of them. Then he became so ill it grew plain he must be left in peace. Except for the physicians and the monks who took him food no one disturbed him, and he lay contemplating the Penitential Psalms, which he had had copied out in very large writing on the walls of his cell, and abandoning himself to weeping. At the end of ten days the parts of Monnica and Patricius which had joined to make his body and soul had weakened and dissolved; and outside the convent the civilisation which was as a body to the soul of Rome and Africa also suffered death. Nothing remained except the Church to which his mother had given him, the Mother Church, where as much of the human tradition was stored as would permit man to repeat in another place the cycle of building up and tearing down, to which, as yet, he has been limited.

BIBLIOGRAPHY

THE number of books by and about Augustine is enormous. The Benedictine edition of the texts, and the new edition issued by Holder of Vienna, are well known; and so too are the English translations of his works published last century by Messrs. Clark of Edinburgh under the editorship of the Reverend Marcus Dods, and by Messrs. Scribner of New York in the Library of Nicene and Post-Nicene Fathers. The seventeenth-century translation of the *Confessions* in the Loeb Library is by far the most enjoyable, but the seventeenth-century translation of *The City of God* is not so useful as that made by the Reverend Marcus Dods. The Letters should be read both in the Loeb and the Clark editions, for each remedies the other's omissions; and the Reverend R. J. Sparrow Simpson's guide to the Letters, which is in the S.P.C.K. 'Handbooks of Christian Literature' series, is very helpful. For the general history of the period one must go to Gibbon, to Bury's *Later Roman Empire,* to Rostovstev's *Social and Economic History of the Roman Empire,* to Volume I. of the *Cambridge Medieval History* (particularly for the pages which disprove the stories about Boniface told by Gibbon), to T. R. Glover's *Life and Letters in the Fourth Century,* and M. Charles Boissier's *La Fin du Paganisme.* For specifically African material there is M. Paul Monceaux's attractive *Histoire Littéraire de l'Afrique chrétienne* and his briefer *Les Africains.* There is also M. J. Toutain's *Les Cités romaines de la Tunisie,* which gives much interesting topographical information about the provinces of Africa Proconsularis, Numidia, and the Mauretanias, which are generally called Roman Africa. Perhaps the best short account of Augustine's life and works is the article by M. E. J. Portalié in the *Catholic Encyclopaedia*. For a popular biography there is M. Louis Bertrand's *Saint Augustin*, which enjoyed a great success just before the war and has been translated into English. It errs on the side of excessively free reconstruction, but it is full of gusto and the author has the advantage of familiarity with Hippo and Thagaste. In spite of appearances, it is greatly preferable to Papini's biography. For an all-round view of Augustine's achievements, *A Monument to St. Augustine,* a volume of essays by various Roman Catholic writers issued to commemorate his fifteenth centenary, is to be recommended. The contributions are unequal in merit, but some, notably those by Monsignor D'Arcy, M. Etienne Gilson, and M. Maurice Blondel, are admirable. M. Gilson's *Introduction à l'Etude de St. Augustin* is not only a most beautiful piece of philosophical writing but has an excellent bibliography, most useful in its list of German works. The part played by Augustine in the building up of the Church is expounded by Harnack from the Protestant point of view in his *History of Dogma* (particularly Volume V.); and there is an interesting but unsympathetic study of him in Professor Eucken's *Die Lebensanschauungen der Grosser Denker* (translated as *The Problem of Human Life as Viewed by Great Thinkers*). This is only a small fraction of Augustinian literature, but it should give the reader a clue to the whole. Among other works which have been consulted for the purpose of this work are Duchesne's *Histoire Ancienne de l'Eglise,* Archbishop Benson's *Cyprian,* Professor Kirk's *The Vision of God,* Dr. Figgis's *Political Aspects of 'The City of God,'* Dr. Mottley's *Studies in the Confessions of St. Augustine,* the Reverend W. Montgomery's *St. Augustine: Aspects of his Life and Work,* Mr. Thomas Whittaker's *Neoplatonism,* M. Louis Grandgeorge's *Augustin et le Néo-platonisme,* M. C. de Boyer's

ST. AUGUSTINE

Christianisme et Néo-platonisme dans la Formation de St. Augustin, M. Bertrand's *Autour de St. Augustin,* Le Nain de Tillemont's *Mémoires des Ecclésiastiques,* Goyau's *Ste. Mélanie,* and the Duc de Broglie's *St. Ambrose.*

INDEX

Abraham, 47
Adam, 47, 109, 121
Adeodatus, son of Augustine, 37, 67, 68, 81, 91
Aesculapius, 23
Albina, 143, 145, 148
Alexandria, 23
Alypius, 16, 17, 60, 64, 66, 71, 77, 78, 81, 83, 143, 144, 147
Ambrose, Bishop of Milan, 55, 56, 57, 58, 59, 60, 64, 69, 73, 78, 81, 82, 92, 100, 104, 105, 115, 143
Anthony, Saint, 75, 76
Apuleius, 31, 32, 42, 131
Aquinas, St. Thomas, 110
Ataulf, 149
Athanasius, 61
Augustine, birth, 12; literary genius, 15-17; relations with family, 17-21, 24-25; early environment, 21-23; conflict between pagans and Christianity, 26-29; schooldays, 30-34; at University of Carthage, 34-38; lives in concubinage, 35-38; loses friend, 38; opinions on art, 38-42; interested in Cicero, 42-43; becomes a Manichæan, 44-51; leaves Manichæanism 52-53; goes to Rome, 54-55; goes to Milan, 55; falls under influence of Ambrose, 55-58; receives Monnica, 59; studies Neo-Platonism, 60-62; plans philosophic life,

63-65; dismisses concubine, 65-72; visits Simplician, 73-74; is converted, 75-79; goes to Cassiciacum, 80-81; is baptized, 81-83; receives vision with Monnica, 84-89; is present at Monnica's death, 89-95; returns to Africa, 96; is made presbyter at Hippo, 97-99; is made bishop, 100; founds theological system, 102-110; discharges episcopal duties, 110-111; correspondence with Jerome, 111-116, 121-123; writes treatise on Labour of Monks, 117; engages in anti-Pelagian controversy, 119-121; writes *The City of God*, 125-129; develops official characteristics, 130-131; engages in anti-Donatist controversy, 132-133, 149-150; entertains Pinian and Melania, 143-149; corresponds with Boniface, 149-150, 154-158; influences modern civilization, 159-162; admonishes clergy, 163; dies, 164-166.
Augustinian monasteries, 96, 99, 101

Boniface, 149, 150, 151, 152, 153, 154, 155, 156, 162, 163
Buddha, 47

INDEX

INDEX

(1)